The Dynamic Congregation

The Dynamic Congregation

A Manual for *Energizing* Your Church

Robert H. Ramey, Jr.

Chalice Press
St. Louis, Missouri

Cover design: Mike Foley
Interior design: Elizabeth Wright
Art Director: Michael Domínguez

This book is printed on acid-free, recycled paper.

Visit Chalice Press on the World Wide Web at
www.chalicepress.com

10 9 8 7 6 5 4 3 2 1 99 00 01 02 03

Library of Congress

Ramey, Robert H. (Robert Homer)
The dynamic congregation : a manual for energizing your church / by Robert H. Ramey, Jr.
p. cm.
Includes bibliographical references.
ISBN 0-8272-0626-7
1. Church renewal. I. Title
BV600.2.R363 1999 99-29736
253—dc21 CIP

Printed in the United States of America

To my father,
Robert H. Ramey, Sr.,
1896–1966,
whose legacy of
honesty,
trust, and
encouragement
continues to
strengthen me.

Contents

Acknowledgments

In many ways this book has required more time and work than anything I have yet written. For one thing, it explores the basic functions of the church, including fellowship, service, proclamation, and celebration. I quickly discovered that it took considerable research and planning to combine the basic functions into a coherent whole. Then, too, as I dealt with each function, it seemed natural to subdivide them into familiar pastoral tasks. The entire process pushed me to reflect critically on twenty-five years of pastoral work, sixteen years of teaching ministry in a theological institution, and more than two hundred seminars with churches and judicatories.

Now, as I look back on this time of reflection and writing, I realize how many people I need to thank. And yet, as some of their names flash through my mind, I see that I will never be able to thank them all. Indeed, some of them would be astonished to know that I am indebted to them! So, at the risk of leaving out many benefactors, I simply mention a few.

C. Benton Kline, Jr., read the chapter on preaching and gave me a number of ideas about organizing the book. Oscar J. Hussel read the chapter on nurture and encouraged me to complete the project. Catherine G. Gonzales, who did not actually read any of the manuscript, informed my work on worship and the sacraments because of the team teaching we did in those subjects at Columbia Theological Seminary in the '90s. Leslie C. Robinson, longtime friend and colleague in ministry, enabled me to think more clearly about the chapters on preaching and worship.

As usual, the students I taught in M.Div., Th.M., and D.Min. programs shaped my thinking. Two of them, Amy Salmon and Mary Villilo, contributed much more than the term papers they wrote for one course, as chapters 3 and 4 of my book readily attest.

The seven churches I served as pastor or interim pastor helped me greatly as they embodied the Pauline concept of the church as the body of Christ. Working with all of them in the basic functions of the church taught me what it means to access the power of the Holy Spirit. Perhaps no church fully became the dynamic organism I envisioned in these pages, yet each one of them contributed to my overall vision, and for that I am grateful.

I am quite indebted to Jon Berquist, Academic Editor at Chalice Press, for his encouragement from beginning to end. His patient manner and incisive analysis always provided just the help I needed.

Once again, I want to thank my wife, Gail, for her support. Often she read the manuscript from the standpoint of the person in the pew and gave me her honest reaction. Then, too, she often doubled as a lay caregiver when the project threatened to overwhelm me!

No perfect church will ever exist, of course, but all of them can become more dynamic and mature. I offer these pages with the hope and prayer that you will feel the wind at your back, indeed the "wind" of the Spirit, blowing where the Spirit wills but always with *power.*

Robert H. Ramey, Jr.
Pinehurst, North Carolina, May 1999

Introduction

Soon in every church—sometimes sooner than later—the proverbial honeymoon ends between pastor and congregation. Antagonists may appear, or ministry becomes dull. Little seems to happen during church services. You eat the bread and drink the wine at communion, even hear in the liturgy that Christ is present, but everyone seems bored. You sit down at yet another potluck dinner and wonder whether the effort is worth it. You call nine people before finding a volunteer to take a meal to a senior citizen. So you mutter at the end of the day, "Is this all our church is ever going to be? This church has no power. Little seems to be happening here."

If as minister, church board member, or congregant, you have ever had such thoughts, you joined company with numerous Christians down through the ages. You suspect that there's more to the Christian faith than such unexciting church life, and you long for the dynamic character of the early Christian community.

I wrote this book because such power is still available to us today. Did not Jesus promise his disciples, "But you will receive power when the Holy Spirit has come upon you" (Acts 1:8)? They received that power, and it changed their lives. Moreover, faithful Christians in every generation since have tapped that same power. And it's open to us now, for the Spirit continues to blow where it will.

Surely the modern church needs that power. Recently I was talking with a psychologist who, with his minister wife, was attending the same retreat as I. He said he often traveled with her to different churches when she did spiritual growth programs. "It makes no difference what denomination the churches belong to," he offered, "they are in sad shape. No life, no vitality."

If what the psychologist said is also true about your church, do not despair. "You will receive power when the Holy Spirit has come upon you," Jesus promised.

So I start with the assumption that the Spirit is still empowering the church today. Now add to that assumption one more: that of the ancient functions or dimensions of the church—fellowship, service, proclamation, and celebration—that continue to define the character of the church. Those activities are etched large on the pages of the New Testament, particularly in the book of Acts; therefore, I will not seek to justify them in detail, for almost anyone interested in reading this book will also stand in the long line of those who accept the validity of those functions.

We first address "being the gospel." *Koinonia*—the common life we share as Christians—is not just one dimension of the church's mission among others. Rather, as Lesslie Newbigin says, the *basic* reality of the church's mission is the creation of a new being through the presence of the Holy Spirit. And he further identifies this new being as the common life *(koinonia)* in the church.[1] From this new creation our service, proclamation, and celebration spring, but our priority is our common life.

When he began his ministry, Jesus appointed twelve apostles "to be with him" (Mk. 3:14). He chose to band together and live out his ministry with a small group of twelve, and occasionally with an even smaller group of Peter, James, and John. He leaned on them for fellowship and support, though they often failed him, as in the garden of Gethsemane.

It was no accident, then, that the early disciples experienced such rich fellowship. After three thousand persons were baptized as a result of Peter's amazing preaching, listen to what they did: "They devoted themselves to the apostles' teaching and *fellowship*" (Acts 2:42a, italics mine). And later, "All who believed were *together*" (Acts 2:44a). They had to be together to share fellowship in and through Jesus Christ.

Whenever you meet with fellow Christians for worship, study, a meal, or a retreat, you share with them in a rich fellowship of those who know Jesus as Lord and Savior. And that fellowship is truly "life together," as Dietrich Bonhoeffer put it,[2] and constitutes fellowship that the world cannot provide.

To deepen our common life, we will set up strategies that enable boards to become faith communities. Moreover, we show how those same boards can provide pastoral care for members in all kinds of distress. Only as church boards and leaders move to create and deepen fellowship—being the gospel—can the church increasingly become a center from which power radiates to the whole church.

So, when fellowship is deep and real, we can then jump to the important task of service: doing the gospel. Doing the gospel also proceeds from fellowship, our common life. Jesus left yet another enduring legacy to the church through his ministry—*diakonia,* service. When his disciples argued about which one of them was the greatest, Jesus told them that the leader must become "like one who serves" (Lk. 22:26b). In fact, he astonished them further by stating, "I am among you as one who serves" (Lk. 22:27b).

At times the early church showed that the example of Jesus was ever before them. All who believed were not only together, as we have seen, but they also "had all things in common; they would sell their possessions and goods and distribute the proceeds to all, as any had need" (Acts 2:45). No doubt such sacrificial actions would startle people today, but can we not assume that people in Jerusalem were just as startled?

Every time you give a cup of water in the name of Jesus, or spend the night in a homeless shelter, or take a brave stand for the gospel, you flesh out what it means to be a servant. *Doing* the gospel has always been a core activity of vital church life. Thus, I will present both a rationale and a model to help churches engage in a social ministry of service and action.

Telling or communicating the gospel, our third function, also proceeds from fellowship. If the church does not demonstrate the reality of the new creation in its common life, its words of proclamation will fall on ears that do not hear.

Surely Jesus "went about all the cities and villages, teaching in their synagogues, and proclaiming the good news of the kingdom" (Mt.9:35a). That's *kerygma,* proclamation, communicating the good news through preaching and teaching.

What Jesus did, the apostles replicated in their practice. When Peter and the apostles were brought before the council in Jerusalem for teaching in the name of Jesus, they once more boldly proclaimed a crucified and risen Savior, concluding with this: "And we are witnesses to these things, and so is the Holy Spirit whom God has given to those who obey him" (Acts 5:32). Even after they were flogged and ordered not to speak in the name of Jesus again, they continued "to teach and proclaim Jesus as the Messiah" (Acts 5:42) in the temple and at home.

Every time you read, proclaim, hear, or teach the gospel, you continue to demonstrate this ancient function of telling the good news. But how can we continue to communicate the faith in an electronic culture in which we increasingly listen with our eyes? Or how can we cultivate the total church as a learning community in an era of declining church attendance? Is it not imperative then for us to look at new models for preaching and teaching the good news in our rapidly changing context?

The final but crucial function remains: celebrating the gospel. We can only celebrate the gospel if we have experienced the new reality in our fellowship. But then, whenever the church gathers to praise God from whom all blessings flow and to meet the risen Christ at his table in the eucharist, it celebrates the gospel—*leitourgia*. When Jesus, "filled with the power of the Spirit" (Lk. 4:14), returned to his hometown of Nazareth, "he went to the synagogue on the sabbath day, as was his custom" (Lk. 4:16). Though Jesus stunned his congregation as he preached on this text from Isaiah, he *worshiped* in the synagogue as he had been trained to do. Surely in all he did he was celebrating the story of God's rule breaking in among them through him.

Life among the first converts in Jerusalem also featured celebrating the gospel. "They devoted themselves to the apostles' teaching and fellowship, *to the breaking of bread and the prayers"* (Acts 2:42b, italics mine). In other words, they celebrated their faith, shared a common meal, including the Lord's supper, and presumably spent time in both their homes and the temple praising God.

When you come together as a fellowship of God's people to celebrate the drama of grace and God's loving justice, you are engaging in an important Christian function. Celebrating, which is closely related to telling the gospel, remains a central activity of the church.

Yet how can people celebrate the gospel if our liturgical jargon sounds to them like a babble of unknown tongues? How can they stand before the baptismal font or the table when they see no connection between their life and the sacraments? Again, stories and models will be given of how churches, in the power of the Spirit, truly reflected the gospel when their congregations met to worship and celebrate the sacraments.

So there you have the functions of being, doing, telling, and celebrating the gospel. These functions depict a church that has become a community of the Holy Spirit, serving any who have need in their own fellowship and in the community, communicating the good news to all who are searching for meaning in a technological age, and gathering often to renew their strength by celebrating the gospel.

But just as Jesus was "filled with the power of the Spirit," and just as the apostles received the power of the Spirit to be witnesses, so too must we pray for the Spirit in our being, doing, telling, and celebrating. Unless we do, much of our functioning will continue to result in our usual wheel-spinning.

Thus, *for a church to be revitalized, two assumptions need to coalesce.* In other words, accessing the power of the Spirit will not be complete unless we particularize that power in the concrete, daily functions of the church. Nor will carrying out the functions of the church be sufficient if not done in the power of the Spirit. Not one or the other—both are necessary.

You will undoubtedly need more help with some of the functions of the church than others. The setting for our work together will be the board meetings of the fictitious Redeemer Church. The board members, typical Christians meeting to lead their church in worship and ministry, will provide the setting for asking some very fundamental questions about the four functions of the church and how the Spirit *might* energize us in each area. I say *might* because the Spirit, like the wind, blows where the Spirit wills. We cannot precisely nail down the movement of the Spirit or click on a computer tool bar to access the power we want. Even so, I am increasingly convinced that the reason so many churches are gasping for air today is not because the Christian faith lacks vitality. Rather, in our churches we have forgotten the source of our power in the Spirit, as well as how we might better carry out the four functions that demonstrate our basic nature as the church of Jesus Christ.

Will it be easy to keep both the Spirit and the four functions of the church in tight focus? No, we will fail again and again. Either we grind away at the tasks of ministry without leaning on the Lord, who said to Zerubbabel long ago, "Not by might, nor by power, but by my spirit" (Zech. 4:6); or we drift along, allowing our telling the gospel to become numbing oratory, being the gospel a superficial meal eaten in the middle of trivial conversation, doing the gospel an infrequent turn at ushering, and celebrating the gospel merely an occasion to feel good about ourselves for going to church.

And that's not enough anymore, as declining membership statistics of mainline churches readily confirm. So we face a massive challenge both to access the source of our power and to revisit the traditional functions of the church. But meeting the challenge will be well worth the effort. Is that not the same task all faithful churches have to address in every age?

The thoughtful reader will quickly see that this book will have to be adapted for each ministry context. Redeemer Church, the setting for this book, is a slowly growing church of 350 members in a small city of 50,000. Obviously, Redeemer's approach to the traditional functions will differ from a small rural church of 100 members or a large church of 1,000 members in a metropolitan area. Nevertheless, the *issues* that Redeemer Church raises are pertinent for all churches, although each church will resolve them differently in light of its own context and resources.

Thus, we embark on the journey before us. Let the board members of Redeemer Church frame relevant questions for us to ask as we travel. I will serve as consultant to the board to assist them as they wrestle with the issues. My greatest hope is for us to experience once again the winds of the Spirit thrusting us forward to faithfully perform the functions of the church as we enter another century in the service of Christ.

Part One

REVITALIZING FELLOWSHIP

Fellowship: Being the Gospel

A New Reality

Fellowship, how easily the word falls from our lips. We talk about the good times we have with friends and family in the workplace, our civic clubs, our neighborhood associations, and our churches. Yet we scarcely understand fellowship in a biblical sense. And that is tragic, since the core issue for church revitalization is fellowship. A biblical understanding embraces several lodestars:

First of all, *the Holy Spirit has created a new reality through Jesus Christ.* This new reality, this new being, this new humanity, this new creation is the common life *(koinonia)* of the church.

Second, *the defining characteristic of the common life of the church is love that "binds everything together in perfect harmony"* (Col. 3:14). In an atmosphere of such love

- persons are accepted as they are
- sin is forgiven
- dividing walls of hostility are broken down
- sisters and brothers live together in harmony and unity

And finally, the church is called to be a sign in and for the world of the new reality that the Holy Spirit has made available in Jesus Christ. Think of it! When the world sees the church, it should see a clear, unmistakable demonstration of a new reality—people-in-community loving, forgiving, breaking down dividing walls of hostility, and living in unity.

Ever experienced such fellowship? If you have, you will surely agree with Paul Minear, who said, "People in this community detected in the works of love that the Spirit produced a primary key to the mystery of ultimate reality."[1] Does not such a phenomenon prove again Paul's daring claim that "God's love has been poured into our hearts through the Holy Spirit that has been given to us" (Rom. 5:5)? Ah, yes. That kind of fellowship is a foretaste of life in heaven, whose citizens we are.

CHAPTER 1

When Church Boards Become Faith Communities

"Tell me about your experience as a board," I asked the leaders of Redeemer Church as we began their annual retreat. "What is it like?"

Soon Maria said, "To tell the truth, our meetings often frustrate me. Sometimes they are so long and conflicted that I find it hard to go to sleep when I get home."

"I no longer expect anything to happen when we meet," Paul quickly added. "We seem to be frozen in time."

"The dynamics of our meetings bother me," said Jan. "We don't work together very well. Some of us, including me, talk too much, while others don't talk at all."

"We're such prisoners of culture," Malcolm added. "I want us to react to issues as Christians who are steeped in the Bible, but we react like Main Street instead."

"Our board concerns me for another reason," added Susan. "Sometimes we don't seem to have a very high opinion of our denomination. If we are asked to study a key issue, for example, we seem to be very suspicious of the denomination's motives. We see things only from the perspective of our little parish."

"It sounds as though we need to take an in-depth look at your work," I concluded.

As both a pastor and a teacher, I had heard the same comments in church after church. *And it was always painful to hear.* Why and how could a group of church leaders, supposedly empowered by the gospel, be so unexcited, frustrated, and bored by their work together? Did their work have to be that way? Isn't there a pathway to renewal for the board and the congregation? And doesn't that pathway begin with the leaders themselves? Surely if leaders are foundering, then the congregation is probably foundering also. Yet several problems, hinted at in our discussion above, block more faithful and productive work.

What's Wrong with Church Boards?

Boards often lack vision for their work. As an older translation of Proverbs puts it, "Where there is no vision, the people perish" (Prov. 29:18, KJV). No wonder many of our churches seem to be dying! We lack vision, which Webster defines as "the ability to perceive something not actually visible, as through mental acuteness or keen foresight."[1]

But why do boards lack the ability to perceive something not actually visible, such as a desired future for their church that is in line with the biblical vision? My first hunch is that the visionary process is hampered by *fear*. Often board members believe that their only responsibility is to guard tradition, both the tradition of their church and that of the Christian faith itself. And they are correct in believing that they should guard tradition.

Yet every board also needs to be open to the Spirit of God, who makes all things new, or else they will become frozen in time, as board member Paul had put it. Herein lies part of our problem: Boards fear that the future may bring unacceptable, unwanted change. Actually, any time someone talks about doing a new thing, homeostasis kicks in because churches, like other systems, want to stay the same. Small churches even fear that new members will rob them of the intimate family feeling they presently have.

My second hunch is that too few board members constantly nourish their visionary power with biblical faith. To be fair, however, the research is not as bleak as one might imagine. In a survey of 4,600 Presbyterians, for example, 50 percent of the elders reported that they had read the Bible individually more than once a month, 22 percent with family, 30 percent in a Bible study group, and 38 percent in another church group.[2] Thus, the picture is by no means hopeless.

Nonetheless, much of what nourishes us all is the incessant impact of culture. Television bombards us with everything from sex and violence to the best cure for heartburn. The marketplace tells us to buy, buy, buy instead of to be, be, be. The community tells us to look out for ourselves first and foremost, even if we have to gate ourselves off from the world. We should hardly wonder, then, whether our spasmodic, mechanical reading of scripture can withstand the overwhelming forces around us. How important it is for us to ground ourselves thoroughly in scripture so that it may shape our vision of where we need to be as a church.

Boards also lack the knowledge they need to do their work well. First of all, they may not possess the basic knowledge they need of their own church government and the duties that they have been assigned. Board member Maria had joined Redeemer Church by transferring from a Baptist Church with congregational governance. It was hard for her not to want to submit every controversial item that came before the board to a vote of the congregation. Further, do not some boards with congregational polities act more like hierarchical churches when basic doctrines are questioned? And do not churches that belong to more hierarchical denominations sometimes act as if they are entities to themselves, maintaining their own programs with little regard for the denomination? Certainly all boards need to study their own system of church governance so that they can be properly guided by it.

Furthermore, boards lack knowledge about basic leadership principles and how they should work together. Isn't it strange that so many board members glibly repeat Jesus' injunction for the leader to become a servant, yet seek to lord it over one another in meetings? (See Lk. 22:27.) Most boards have key persons who, when they speak, find that everybody listens. And votes accordingly! Malcolm, a respected banker in the community, was such a leader at Redeemer Church. Numerous other board members who could contribute helpfully seldom speak. Or when they do, the board may ignore them. The church is the body of Christ, seeking to utilize the spiritual gifts of all, yet we stress the gifts of the few.

Transforming Boards into Faith Communities

While working with the board of Redeemer Church, I made four suggestions for renewing their work. Other boards can follow the suggestions sequentially as time and energy permit. See how they can be helpful in your church.

Cultivate a deliberate plan for spiritual growth among board members. Church leaders want to grow in grace and to become more effective in their ministry. While leading retreats for church leaders, I have been impressed by the seriousness with which most of them address their responsibilities. However, part of their problem lies in how they have been trained for board work. Almost all denominations provide some training for their board members, examining their personal experience, their knowledge of the church and its tradition, and their leadership duties.

Yet after being installed in their positions, few leaders know how to continue maturing. When they attend board meetings, all of their energy flows into managing leaky faucets and coordinating the church calendar. Little if any time is devoted to helping leaders reflect on their lives in Christ and their ministry in the world. Opening and closing meetings with prayer is hardly enough. No wonder so many leaders tire of board work, saying, "I can't wait until my term is up!" They cannot keep on serving with unflagging zeal if their spiritual well runs dry. To cultivate spiritual growth, follow a two-step process:

Ask board members to fill out the spirituality wheel to determine their spiritual type. Corinne Ware has constructed this useful inventory, which is based on the work of Urban T. Holmes.[3] On its vertical axis the inventory measures how we *know*, whether by *intellectualizing* or by *feeling* and intuition. On its horizontal axis it reveals how we *pray and meditate,* whether by *imagining* God concretely as knowable or by *emptying* the mind before God as mystery. The wheel separates persons into four quadrants, showing that we have predominant tendencies toward either thinking, feeling, being, or doing. Of course, we all possess multiple tendencies, although we favor one way of learning and praying over another.

In using the spirituality wheel with dozens of groups, I have seen how quickly persons understand their diversity in both their personal and congregational preferences. The inventory shows why one person wants more Bible study, while another prefers to pray in solitude. As well, it shows why one person wants to praise the Lord all the time, while another says, "My work is my prayer." When boards discover these differences about who they are, they readily see several benefits. The boards

- see why they often differ on the types of programs and worship patterns they develop
- begin to listen more intently to the proposals others make when they see that their spirituality has a valid and significant history
- learn different spiritual practices from others
- begin to make space in their congregation for the differences of other people so that *all* members can continue to grow spiritually

For example, boards will more likely provide opportunities for persons who cherish solitude and want to engage in contemplation and meditation. Just because most members practice more rational ways of communicating with God does not mean that everyone communicates that way. Likewise, boards of congregations that are more expressive in their praise of God may channel some of that energy into concrete service projects, such as Habitat for Humanity. Thus, persons in the minority not only will grow but will feel more part of the congregation and enrich its life. Otherwise, they may feel left out and soon drift into inactivity or on to another church.

Etched in my memory is a conversation I had at the church door after a sermon I once preached on the charismatic movement. Instead of blindly condemning the movement, I attempted to explain its significance and to show how it can help the church. A parishioner said to me, "Thank you for that sermon. Now I feel so normal!" Before then she had felt uncomfortable and unaccepted, sensing only that she was in the minority in her spiritual preferences.

After board members have identified their spiritual types, ***ask them to study the biblical characteristics that early Christian leaders embodied.*** In the book of Acts, we find that leaders were chosen because they:

- were called to office by God's providence
- possessed a Christian experience
- bore witness to the Christian message
- were empowered by the Holy Spirit
- served as examples of the Christian faith
- received the approval of the Christian community, and
- served in order to lead[4]

The earliest Christians chose leaders not necessarily because they were popular, or influential, or big contributors. Rather, they chose them because they embodied the Christian faith. Granted, people who are popular, influential, and wealthy may embody those biblical characteristics. Board member Jan of Redeemer Church was a popular leader in her community, but more importantly, members regarded her as a mature Christian. When selecting leaders today, we must choose persons who similarly flesh out the above characteristics and help them continue to mature.

Next, it's important for leaders to reflect on whether they are growing in those leadership qualities. Most of them want to grow but either don't know how or become bogged down in the "busyness" of church life. "My Personal Rule of Life" in appendix A has been designed so that leaders can mark the practices they are willing to follow in order to mature in their faith. Encourage them *not* to select too many practices or disciplines, lest they soon become discouraged. I also invite them to declare their intentions to someone else or to a small group—a shared declaration always reinforces new intentions. Then I ask them to become mutually accountable to one another for the practice of these disciplines. Few people are so disciplined that they can hold themselves accountable without the help of others. So spend time at every board meeting talking about spiritual growth and its necessity for faithful, continuing service in the church.

By all means, leaders should see that their growth in grace will never be automatic. The practices they employ are not magic growth pills. Yet by faithfully engaging in them day by day, they position themselves to receive God's amazing grace.

Tap the immense power that lies in storytelling and history-giving in light of the biblical story. "Tell me your faith story," you may ask them individually. Corporately you may ask, "What is the 'founding story' of this church?"

When I first heard Al's story, it was so powerful I could hardly speak. He described his life as active, filled with many projects, and yet unsatisfying. Late one night he prayed, "Lord, I don't want to be hungry and thirsty anymore." Soon, he said, he was filled with a peace he had never had before. Everyone could see that Al was changed. He had a new zeal for his work, a new vision for the church, and boundless energy. We could see that the God who was active in the exodus and exile was also active in Al's life now. Such stories always inspire and motivate coworkers.

Are we focusing too much on personal experience as we seek the renewal of board life? There is often a danger that we will become so absorbed in our stories that we will forget to focus on the Bible and what it says about who God is and what God requires of us. Shirley Guthrie reminds us that in the Bible we discover that "the Holy Spirit is the Spirit of a God who cares for each of us, knows better than we what we need most, and promises to be present and at work in our lives just as we *give up* self-centered preoccupation with ourselves and our little life stories to remember who it is from whom our help comes."[5] And yet, we dare not forget that our life stories have tremendous power to build community, to establish our identity, and to energize our work both as individuals and as boards. When we look at our stories in light of the Story, we can discern how God has been at work. We see who God is from what God has done. We tell our stories not to laud ourselves but to glorify God, who has cared for us every day of our lives. From telling our personal stories it's only one short step to telling the congregation's story, also essential for effective work.

When congregations give their histories, they are almost always amazing. At the Redeemer Church retreat I asked them to tell their founding story. It seems that a ten-year-old girl named Dorothy had asked her mother one morning, "Mommy, why do we have to drive so far to church. Couldn't we have a church here?" Her mother, clearly surprised, said, "Dorothy, I don't know why we don't have a church here, but I'll find out." Dorothy's mother asked several other church members the same question Dorothy asked her. They didn't know either but agreed to meet to explore the possibility of a new church in their community. It did not take long for them to go to their denominational officials and start a year-long process that led to a new church development. All because Dorothy asked a question out of her child-like curiosity, and her mother listened.

Even so, is it not astonishing that so many boards reject storytelling and history-giving as a waste of time? Charles M. Olsen reports that 605 Presbyterian elders across the country were asked: "How often did each of the following events or actions take place while you were on the session?" *Sharing faith stories and reviewing church stories/history ranked at the bottom of an optional list of fourteen choices.* Not only that, when asked whether sharing both their faith and church stories would make serving on the session more meaningful, responses ranked them eleventh and twelfth out of a possible fourteen choices. More than one third did not think stories and history even have a place on the agenda of a board meeting.[6] No doubt, some denominations would probably have responded more favorably to storytelling and history-giving, but Presbyterians are not alone in resisting the practice.

Evaluate board work by whether it is a sign, a foretaste, and an instrument of God's reign. This third step toward renewal actually flows from the previous step, growing in grace. If board members are maturing in biblical faith, they will have the depth they need to analyze their work by biblical criteria. Unless they do, they will continue to evaluate what they do by cultural standards that are often contrary to the gospel, thereby illustrating board member Malcolm's problem with the Redeemer board.

Church work is supposed to be a *sign* of God's reign. In other words, the church points to the life, death, and resurrection of Jesus Christ. Is the church not required to direct people toward the power and love of God, not self-righteously toward itself? After all, as God's own people, the church proclaims the mighty acts of God who called us "out of darkness into his marvelous light" (1 Pet. 2:9b).

Through its *worship* and *ministry* the church acts as a sign of God's rule. In its worship the church gathers to read, hear, and faithfully proclaim the Word. In its ministry the church reaches out to the poor and oppressed, works for peace and justice, and cares for God's creation. Thus, one criterion by which a church judges its worship and ministry is this: By this action are we serving as a sign of God's rule?

As Redeemer board members thought about their Sunday services, they asked, "Does what we do here indicate that we are responding to God's word? Does our liturgy point to the kingdom?" When they were ruthlessly honest, they admitted that often their services did not meet the test. Al said, "I believe most of what we do is designed to make people feel good instead of helping them to trust God. I can't tell much difference between what we do at worship and what my civic club does." The Redeemer board saw that in order to be a sign of the kingdom more was involved than making people feel good.

Further, is not the church supposed to be a *foretaste* of God's rule? A foretaste is an appetizer before the real meal. Our life in the church, then, is an appetizer that precedes the messianic banquet of our Lord. We sample this appetizer in our church fellowship at potluck dinners. We experience it when we forgive one another. We encounter it every time we are accepted in our human frailty. Such moments may be all too rare, but when they happen we know we have found meaning and hope.

Of course, the foretaste we have experienced is *only* an appetizer. For has not the church often failed to forgive, accept, and offer meaning and hope? In my long ministry I have been rocked frequently by stories of wounded ministers and crushed laypersons who were hurt by the church. Every reader can offer abundant evidence of such failures. Christians, therefore, should engage in no illusions about the quality of our fellowship. Still, times of significance have broken through for all of us, or else I would not be writing this book and you would not be reading it. The church, despite its spotty record, has given us enough appetizers along the way to stimulate us to long for the main dinner in the life to come. Meanwhile, the appetizer is the foretaste we need to strengthen us as we lead our churches. So we must ask again and again whether our life together accurately mirrors life in the kingdom.

When I asked board members if Redeemer Church was a foretaste of God's reign, they paused for a long time. Finally, Amanda said, "I wish we were, but when I first came to this church, I recall an awkward moment in a Sunday school class I attended. As we discussed the passage on love in 1 Corinthians, I said that I had become disillusioned about love since my divorce. There was dead silence before someone changed the subject. Their message to me was: 'We don't talk about divorce in this class.' I almost left the church as a result." Redeemer Church wanted to be a foretaste of the kingdom, yet they admitted that their actions sometimes left only a bitter taste.

It's also crucial to evaluate church life by whether it's an *instrument* of God's rule. Jesus enjoins us to preach good news to the poor, to proclaim release to the captives and recovery of sight to the blind, and to let the oppressed go free. (See Lk. 4:18–20.) He has told us to visit those in prison, feed the hungry, give drink to the thirsty, and clothe the naked. (See Mt. 25:31–46.) Even now Jesus sends us out to practice such ministry. We are to be *instruments* of God's reign.

So we launch out in our worship and ministry to join God in what God is doing in the world. God cares about the homeless and the prisoner. God cares about those who have been battered by bullies and molested by warped persons. God cares about families who lose a loved one in a crash caused by a drunk driver who has already been arrested twice. God cares about the elderly who sit in nursing homes, lonely and waiting to die. God cares about children working long hours in sweatshops around the world. *At the doorstep of every church lie a host of opportunities for that church to be an instrument of God's love.*

When Redeemer Church considered that criterion, they immediately saw that they had been concerned only about serving themselves. Since they had almost no outreach ministry, they set about discovering root needs in the community that no one else was meeting. Low cost, affordable housing surfaced at once as a root need and will be discussed later.

Let's add a third criterion to the way churches evaluate their work: serving and witnessing as instruments of God's rule. These three criteria give us yardsticks, both to measure our present life and also to gauge new proposals that come to the table of every board.

Employ tools to improve board relationships. Already we have seen how the spirituality wheel promotes respect for others' spirituality. When leaders cultivate a plan for growing spiritually, their ability to work with one another will improve, sometimes dramatically. Such improvement flows directly from the gospel itself and the ancient disciplines like prayer and scripture study that have always nourished and empowered Christians in every century.

Other tools, such as the Myers-Briggs Type Indicator (MBTI), can also help us. Actually, the MBTI and the spirituality wheel can be juxtaposed in certain, but not all, ways. Takers of the MBTI fit into one of sixteen different personality profiles. Though perhaps used too much and critiqued too little, the MBTI can increase our interpersonal understanding and greatly improve working relationships in small groups, including boards. This tool usually confirms how we feel about ourselves and other people with whom we are working.

When I took the MBTI, I scored as an ESFJ. I discovered that I favor extraversion over introversion, that I am more sensing than intuitive, more feeling than thinking, and more judging than perceiving. Thus, I immediately saw why people energize me more than solitude, why I favor following experience over intuition, why I find it difficult to make personal decisions on the basis of sheer rationality, and why I like to have our travel plans nailed down when I leave home. Those have been significant learnings for me, and I have observed those learnings to be significant for hundreds of others also. And these learnings transfer directly to our church boards. At once we see why some people talk more than others, or find it difficult to take decisive action about a church employee, or struggle to make long-range plans. Granted, understanding these interpersonal dynamics is only the first step. It does not automatically mean we will start working better as a board. But when we begin with a deeper understanding of one another, we can then work together more effectively to reach consensus about the decisions we make.

And yet, do not use the MBTI uncritically or exclusively. Some people see it only as one tool among others to use in studying our personalities, while others question whether it has enough empirical support. Still others observe that "the MBTI profiles read like horoscopes from Camelot, failing to see that from a Christian perspective our humanity is far more complex and flawed than the sixteen profiles reveal."[7] While each of the above reservations is partly valid, especially the latter, church boards can still profitably employ the MBTI. It always seems to cause persons to say, "Aha, now I understand myself and others better."

As I have written elsewhere, *servant leadership* needs to define and characterize Christian leadership.[8] Did not Jesus say for leaders to become servants? Did he not model that behavior by washing his disciples' feet and by standing before them, saying, "I am among you as one who serves?"

In my work with church boards I have found that most of them subscribe to servanthood theoretically. Yet in the rough-and-tumble of board life, they don't know how to function like servants—they need to see how to flesh it out in their work. So I invite them to consider six leadership qualities identified by Rensis Likert and pioneered by the Center for Parish Development.[9]

To summarize, leaders need to *act supportively* so that persons will see that they are appreciated and affirmed. Leaders *are open and receptive to new ideas*, showing persons that they value both them and their ideas whether they agree with them or not. Leaders *spend time in team building,* believing that all members have gifts and talents that will contribute to productivity and enhance personal relationships. Leaders *help members with their work,* knowing that indifference is likely to turn people off. Leaders *expect excellence and model excellence,* knowing that mediocrity in expectation and behavior will produce mediocrity. And leaders *use group methods of decision making,* showing that they want to reach consensus as they are guided by the Holy Spirit. Those leadership qualities give flesh and blood to what Jesus meant by servant leadership. *Growing in servant leadership always helps a board do its work better.*

Becoming a Growing Faith Community: One Church's Story

Fortunately, the Redeemer board set aside enough time at the retreat to discuss my four suggestions. Important in my concluding statements was an adaptation of an old Lithuanian proverb: "If you keep on doing what you're doing, you'll keep on getting what you're getting." The profound implications of this simple proverb began to sink in. Members saw that if they didn't make significant changes in the way they "did board," they would keep on getting what they had been getting: boredom, fatigue, disappointment, and long, unproductive meetings. Moreover, they would keep on providing uninspiring leadership.

The board members also saw that if they kept on doing in their personal lives what they had been doing, they would keep on getting what they had been getting: little spiritual growth. So I asked them to ponder whether they really wanted to change, knowing that nothing would happen if they kept on doing what they were doing.

After reviewing my suggestions for transformation, the board of Redeemer Church decided to take action. They first determined that they would cultivate their spiritual growth. While still at the retreat, they carefully read "My Personal Rule of Life," marking a practice or two in each section that they agreed to follow. (See appendix A.) The sections correspond with the quadrants of the spirituality wheel and thus provided them with concrete ways to grow in faith.

Next, I asked board members to fill out an inventory by Gerald May, listing possible impediments to developing spiritual awareness. (See appendix B.) May's broad list ranges from "Don't know how to do it" to "Too much on my mind." In the plenary that followed, board members gave a variety of responses about why cultivating spiritual awareness was so difficult. Their most frequent answers:

1. "Fear of (various things)."
2. "Need to be *doing* something."

3. "Can't find the time."
4. "Don't know how to do it."
5. "Other more important things."

An intense discussion followed as we tried to deal constructively with each impediment for practicing their chosen disciplines. When I highlighted their ongoing need to become mutually accountable to one another for such practice, they adopted a twofold plan. First, they agreed to discuss their progress at every board meeting, reporting failures as well as successes. The second aspect they approved was to discuss—and practice, when possible—a new discipline at each meeting. Al volunteered to lead the first discussion on prayer.

The board made another key decision about storytelling and history-giving. At each meeting, one of their members would share his or her personal faith story, allowing time for persons to respond with affirmation and/or questions. The purpose was to understand how the Holy Spirit, who had guided and sustained each one of them individually, would also guide and sustain them corporately as a board.

Finally, the board members realized that there was no quick fix to transformation. Rather, they planned gradual steps to enable themselves to become more fully a faith community. Aware of their need to work more effectively, they decided to schedule another meeting each quarter to examine their working relationships in light of their spiritual growth. A committee was appointed to explore the merits of using the Myers-Briggs Type Indicator as a tool to promote better working relationships.

The Redeemer board was soon deep into its renewal program, realizing that such renewal was essential for revitalizing the congregation. At once, ideas for their ongoing work tumbled out. "When a board is renewed, can we continue to give pastoral care as before?" asked board member Steve. Steve's question now leads us to address another important subject: caregiving in the church.

CHAPTER 2

Caregiving as a Sign of the New Reality

"Who gives pastoral care in your church?" I asked the board members of Redeemer Church at their first quarterly meeting.

"Quite honestly," replied Justin, who had been pastor of the church for four years, "I give most of the official care in my parish. And actually I think people like it that way. Sometimes I exhort our board to care for the sick, the grieving, and the lonely, but I think most people regard it as my responsibility."

"Well," said Amanda, "I think we would like to help, but we haven't had the training you have received. Besides, some members of the church wouldn't want us to know about their hurts and needs, and they would share them with you."

"We all give some pastoral care individually to people in the church as the need arises," said Jan. "We just don't have a corporate understanding of what we need to do as a board."

"To be realistic," said Al, "my home church in rural Maryland sometimes astonished me by its love. When someone died, the church supported the grieving family in amazing ways—food and more food, telephone answerers—you name the need, our people met it. But there were other needs that went begging, as when a divorce occurred. Now in this larger church, we leave much of the pastoral care to Justin. No one seems to know what to do about it."

"And what has been the net result?" I asked.

"I'm tired," laughed Justin. "And I know I have to do something to train others to give pastoral care. If I don't, I fear I will eventually burn out. I don't want that to happen!"

"Nor do we," added Steve.

Ministry Belongs to All Members

The dilemma of the Redeemer Church board was not new to me—I had heard it often—but each time I hear it, it hits me like a sledgehammer. Always I wonder, "How did the church end up in this predicament? Isn't the church the people of God? The new creation? The fellowship in faith? And the body of Christ himself?[1] How then did members of the church come to believe that only clergy should give pastoral care? And that strangers and divorcees should not be loved and accepted?"

Actually, most readers of this book already know some of the history behind the clergy-lay split. We know, for example, that early on all Christians belonged to the *laos*, the people of God. Only later were clergy overseers (elders and bishops) added to local churches.[2] "The real work of ministry (care for widows and orphans, tending to the spiritual needs of the sick, basic instruction, and probably considerable preaching) was the work of deacons and the lay church members. The apostles and others moved in a wide geographical area proclaiming and interpreting the Resurrection. Presumably, bishops and elders became leaders and overseers for a larger town or region."[3]

Gradually, for reasons not entirely clear, pastoral oversight and decision making shifted more and more to the clergy. Even though Reformers like Luther and Calvin, and later Wesley in England, stressed the role of the laity, the clergy-lay split remains to this day.

Now, in our minds we know that laity and clergy differ not in status but in function, and even those functional differences are blurred and often debated. *Yet we continue to act as though the context for all lay ministry is the congregation, not the world.* So why should we even consider lay pastoral care in the congregation? Does that not in itself perpetuate a false understanding of the real context for lay ministry? In one sense, yes. For it seems to say that if we foster lay pastoral care, we will therefore further the ministry of the laity. And we know that we need to do much more than that to develop a rich and full concept of laity serving Christ in all of life.

But wait. The crucial context for lay ministry is in the world, as we shall see later. For now, simply note at least one emerging trend: Laity are increasingly giving pastoral care in the congregation. Even that trend will help laity in their principal ministry arena in the world. For example, if they learn to listen intently to a troubled person in the congregation, will that not help them listen better to a spouse or troubled teenager in their homes? If they learn to love people in the congregation just as they are, will that not help them to go and do likewise in the workplace? Granted, such learning does not automatically transfer to another setting. All pastors know how *we* can concentrate on what a grieving person is saying at church only to go home and bury our heads in a newspaper when our spouse speaks!

Honesty compels most clergy to admit that they know better. They know that members spend far more time living their lives outside the walls of the church than inside. But clergy still encourage them to spend more time inside the walls doing "church work." Spending more time inside the church would be worth it if laity were being trained for their work in the world. Yet that is hardly the case. Inevitably, clergy get caught up in maintaining ministry, not promoting mission. It's so easy to see the need for ushers, a choir, Sunday school teachers, board members, and secretaries, but more difficult to keep in focus *why* we need all those people! We need them in those roles on a limited basis to help all members function faithfully and effectively on a full-time basis as witnesses of Christ *in the world.*

Still, laity can give pastoral care and thereby achieve two purposes. They will (1) begin to return ministry to a shared function; and (2) help people know that they are loved, accepted, and forgiven, and thus part of the new reality. And until the church becomes the new reality, it can hardly do, tell, and celebrate the gospel of Jesus Christ.

A Model for Training Laity to Give Pastoral Care

Where do church leaders start? For example, do you start training your official board or do you select church members who are gifted in the area of giving pastoral care? It depends on a couple of variables.

First, answer a prior question: What are the official duties of your board? Is your board formally charged to "visit and comfort and care for the people, with special attention to the poor, the sick, the lonely, and those who are oppressed"?[4] Those explicit instructions for elders are written into the constitution of my denomination. Other denominations mandate similar instructions. If so, begin here as you seek to "contribute to the needs of the saints" (Rom. 12:13a). Later, you can expand this ministry to include others, especially those in the congregation whom you discern to possess the gift of caring.

A sticky wicket: Do you train board members or Stephen ministers? One phenomenon sweeping across the church landscape has been the Stephen Ministry program. Though I have never undergone the training, I have talked with many ministers and laypersons who have. Uniformly they report a high-quality program that offers excellent training for caregivers. So here is an invaluable resource for those churches who are looking for ways to train caregivers.

However, an interesting question emerges. In denominations that select, even ordain, persons to diaconal ministries, why start another group called Stephen Ministers? In other words, if deacons are already in place and charged "to minister to those who are in need, to the sick, to the friendless, and to any who may be in distress,"[5] why not train *them*? Why set up another order of caregivers when you haven't trained the first group? Of course, a church could always offer its deacons the training of the Stephen Ministry program. The same point also applies to sessions of elders in some denominations, for they are charged "to visit and comfort and care for the people."[6]

Perhaps the key task for every church is to put in place a group that needs to be trained to give pastoral care. If so, at least try to train that group before creating another entity to do the same thing! My hunch is that we haven't tried and failed, we simply haven't tried.

The main difficulty that most church boards report is that the administrative load overwhelms them.[7] They simply don't have enough time and energy left to undertake quality pastoral care. Yet I am not persuaded. In working with boards as a pastor in five different churches, I must admit that we sometimes did not take our pastoral responsibility as seriously as we did boilers and budgets! Nor did we allow spirituality to transform administration. Curious, isn't it, that neither pastoral concerns nor spirituality have informed and reformed our board work very much? Therein may lie part of the reason for the widespread burnout and/or disillusionment of board members after serving a term or two. Could not training boards to carry out their official pastoral duties give them more meaning and excitement?

So, whom do you train to give pastoral care? Start with those who are supposed to give it.

Essentials for a Lay Pastoral Care Program

Many pastors themselves can provide the in-depth training needed for this task. Most seminaries have already provided them with excellent clinical pastoral education. In my pastorates I sometimes went over the basic principles of hospital visitation so that our board members would not make thoughtless and hurtful mistakes. More than once I told them not to sit on a hospital patient's bed or to stay for a long visit. Simple things, yes, but often overlooked by the untrained.

If you as a pastor are in charge of the training program, familiarize yourself with some of the basic resources in the field. Howard W. Stone's early work, titled *The Caring Church: A Guide for Lay Pastoral Care,* is extremely helpful in supplying basic content about the nature of pastoral visits.[8] Kenneth Haugk, founder of the Stephen series of lay caring ministry, condensed some key insights of the Stephen program in *Christian Caregiving: A Way of Life,* and he also furnished a helpful guide for leaders.[9]

The Redeemer Board Goes to Work

The Redeemer board met for a brainstorming session on pastoral care. Pastor Justin himself was the right person to train his board members. Not only was he a good pastor, but he also had recently enrolled in a Doctor of Ministry program in which he took a supervised unit of pastoral care. He looked forward to training the laity for pastoral care, regarding it as a further opportunity for sharing ministry. "Who in our congregation needs care at this time?" Justin asked.

After a slow start, answers from the board members poured forth in a torrent:

"Suzanne has just gone through a divorce."

"Wendy has a new baby."

"Frank lost his job when his company downsized."

"The Bartletts are now empty nesters."

"Jane is going to the Mayo Clinic for further tests."

"Bill has been drinking heavily and was recently arrested for drunk driving."

"Troy and Anna's daughter has just moved to Denver."

"Which of these needs are *socially acceptable* and invite a visit or phone call?" Justin then asked. "Which of them are *socially unacceptable* and make us cautious about visiting? And which of them are *borderline* cases?" As the board responded, Justin compiled three lists on the chalkboard, reserving the third list for socially questionable problems. Quickly it became apparent that an illness, a death in the family, or an impending move were socially acceptable problems. But it also became evident that alcoholism, attempted suicides, marital problems, or teenage pregnancies were needs that could be accompanied by social rejection, because some persons do not find them to be acceptable needs. The third list contained borderline difficulties such as losing a job or suffering from mental illness. Thus, some problems obviously invited concern, others caused embarrassment and discomfort, while still others raised considerable doubt about how the church should respond. When the discussion ended, board members had gained a better idea of when to respond to needs and when to be more tentative. They also decided something else: When in doubt, it's usually better to do something than nothing.

In reviewing their work, Pastor Justin noted another way to categorize pastoral need. He said that we are to give care in illness, particularly during terminal illness. Certainly we give care at death. He also pointed out that other key losses in life create much pain and necessitate congregational care and support, including job loss or the loss of an important relationship. Justin further highlighted the need for care in broken relationships that are characterized by sin and the need for forgiveness. And finally he noted the necessity to care for others in the transitions of life, when children leave home or aging parents become dependent; when people begin work or start households; or when they change jobs or move to new locations.

Justin next focused on fundamental skills that all caregivers need. The principles clustered in three areas: the need to understand human behavior, the principles of caregiving, and the helping resources of the Christian faith. The substance of his teaching follows.

Understanding Human Behavior

All behavior has meaning. Although we may not know what lies behind human actions, there's a reason for it. Being aware of this principle has saved me from misjudgment on many occasions. In an early pastorate I recall a visit I made to a young family in the congregation. During the visit, little Johnny kept trying to speak, but his parents always said, "Quiet, Johnny!" Then suddenly the TV came on with a loud blast. The parents jumped all over Johnny, saying, "Haven't we told you a thousand times not to interrupt us when we're talking?" But Johnny chose to have that kind of attention rather than none at all.

People develop certain patterns of living and stick with them. Change is always possible, of course, but we tend to live out our early patterns for better or worse. A shy person goes to meeting after meeting, saying each time, "I'm gonna speak up this time," but never does. The verbose person also attends meeting after meeting, saying, "I'm not gonna speak so often," but always does. The alcoholic reaches for another drink, saying, "This is my last drink. I really mean it this time." But you know the rest of that story.

Although we may intend to be different and to act differently, our willpower becomes enslaved to the point that we cry out with the apostle Paul, "Wretched man that I am! Who will rescue me from this body of death?" (Rom. 7:24). When we realize that persons tend to live out their behavior patterns, we then may withhold our glib advice about what they should do or how they should feel. That in itself is a major learning for the caregiver.

People react to life as they see it, not as we see it. Although perhaps we should know better, we often dump our life perspectives on others instead of listening to theirs. We seem convinced that *we* have the correct answer to everyone's problems! I see this often when flying. Routine flights have never bothered me much. However, I have sometimes noticed anxious looks on the faces of others seated around me. I want to turn and say to them, "This plane has been built to fly. It will withstand a lot of turbulence. And, besides, you were in more danger riding to the airport today than you are in this plane." But my scared passenger friends are reacting to the situation as *they* see it, not as *I* see it. They do not feel in control, and my rational approach has no effect on them whatever. Thus, to be helpful, caregivers must put themselves in the shoes of others and try to see life as they see it.

Understanding the Principles of Caregiving

Know when to offer help. Certain situations invite your help—grief is a prime example. When people are grieving, it is acceptable to visit, send food, write a card, or phone. Not responding leaves most people feeling, "Will I be left here to mourn alone?"

Other situations are more problematic. If the need is socially unacceptable—like alcoholism—you don't have an automatic invitation to respond. Instead, you are left wondering, "Do I have the right to go? Will I be perceived as a busybody? Will I be invading someone's privacy?" While no one can give a generic prescription for all situations, it's better to take the risk of going than not going. Just be prepared for possible failure, and don't let that stop you from taking action in the future.

Know how to give help when you go. In awkward cases, one can say simply, "If I can be of help in light of what has happened, if indeed anything has happened at all, I'll be glad to try." Whereupon the other person can respond in one of several ways. He can brush you off by saying, "I did get plastered at the party, but I'm okay now. How have you been?" Or she may remark, "What on earth are you talking about? Who have you been talking to, anyway?" which will make you feel battered and rejected unless you once put up the same kind of denial in similar circumstances. Or he can become teary-eyed, collapse, and reply,

"Thank God you're here. I really need help." Such varied responses are unpredictable, yet their unpredictability should not prevent our concern.

Initially attempt to *achieve contact with the person,* as Howard Stone puts it.[10] Establish rapport, hoping that you will be able to go further. When someone collapses and asks for help, you have already achieved contact, or else the person would not invite further help. Identify with persons where they are, not where you would like them to be. Acceptance, acceptance! So easy to say, so hard to do. It begins with putting yourself into the frame of reference of others, attempting to see life as they see it.

Provide a caring presence for people. We would do well to reverse an old proverb and say: Don't just do something, stand there! Or sit there. Still, when others are suffering, we think we must fill up the space with words, words, and more words. Either the silence makes us uncomfortable, or we think we have to fix the problem.

For starters, we try words of *reassurance*: "The sun will shine tomorrow." Then we speak words of *argumentation*: "Do you realize how much you have to be thankful for?" Next we try *platitudes*: "You made this bed; now you must lie in it." Then we offer words of *evaluation*: "That was a dumb thing to do!" Words of *interpretation* may follow: "Hm, I wonder if that problem could stem from your childhood." We can seldom resist giving words of *advice:* "If I were you, I would stop feeling sorry for myself." And finally we love to share words about our *experience*: "Now, let me tell you about my operation."

All of us who have suffered uniformly report that we would have been helped much more if our Christian friends had just shut up and sat there with us, listening sympathetically, even listening to the sound of our silence.

We know well the difference it makes when others actively listen to us, and when they listen unattentively. Active listening—"I'm with you in your struggle all the way"—turns us on. All who struggle need that. Inattentive listening—"I'll endure this tale of woe with muffled ears and glassy eyes"—turns us off. No one needs that.

A caring presence and active listening require us to listen for feelings involved in what others are saying. Are they angry, sad, happy? Feelings indicate the importance to us of what we are saying. Often we talk about ourselves without being aware of our feelings. I once heard someone pound his desk while exclaiming, "I am not angry!"

Also, surmise the content or substance of others' needs as well. Is he angry because he is threatened with losing his job? In this process, attempt to *boil it down,* as Howard Stone also suggests.[11] Frequently people talk all around a problem without focusing on what is bothering them. As people talk with radio therapist Dr. Laura, they often hear her ask, "What then is your problem?" It's sometimes difficult to tell because callers talk about their problems without clearly identifying what they are.

Finally, help other persons cope actively with the presenting difficulty.[12] You are not there to provide a "quick fix" for anyone. But through your caring presence you can offer the support others need to learn how to cope. Be slow to give advice. If you aren't, you take away the person's responsibility to make his or her own decisions. Also, if the decision backfires, you may be blamed. As people talk, seeking the guidance of the Holy Spirit, solutions pop into awareness that were not apparent at first.

Still, there are times when we ask, "What further can I do to help?" This question invites people to continue the relationship or to receive concrete help, depending on the circumstances. An elderly husband who is caring for his invalid wife may request that you sit with her or go to the grocery store to pick up a few items.

In the end, you hope and pray that your help will be truly helpful. "Bear one another's burdens,"said Paul (Gal. 6:2a), but he later added, "all must carry their own loads" (Gal. 6:5). As a caregiver, then, stand supportively with people so that the burden does not overwhelm them. Yet when you stand with them, you encourage them to shoulder their own loads. We dare not assume responsibility for anyone else's life. So build rapport with people, try to get to the essence of their problem, and then help them deal with it constructively.[13]

Caregiving is an art, to be sure, but it's an art that can be learned, with hard work and patience. Reflect on your caregiving to see what went right and what went wrong. Talk it over with others who are giving care also. There's no substitute for reflection on your practice of the art.

Does one ever give up in face of difficult situations? Yes and no. Yes, when you realize you're in over your head, as when someone begins to talk about deep family dysfunction. No, in the sense that you never abandon the person. Although you may be unable to offer the *primary* help needed, you can offer *secondary* support through continuing interest and prayers. In working with many church families over the years, I gradually realized when I could offer primary help and when I should offer secondary help only. And that should be the pattern for lay caregivers as well. Your main task is to find the right help for people, not to give the primary help.

Using the Resources of the Christian Faith

Obviously, some of the above advice has been informed by current psychology and psychiatry. The church has learned much from those sciences, and I am in their debt also. But all too often the church has neglected its own strong resources for healing and health. Only now are we seeing the restoration of the proper balance between learning from other disciplines and the Christian faith itself.

Take *prayer*, for example. Of course, you can misuse prayer by preaching to people or saying things you left unsaid in your conversation! Or you can ask people to pray with you when you are uncomfortable and want to bring closure to a visit. Yet prayer, rightly understood, can be a meaningful resource for you as caregiver and for the "helpee" as well. God cares about us as individuals. God is with us when two or three meet together in Christ's name. And God answers prayer, incorporating our prayers into the divine will. Is that not a stunning resource for every Christian caregiver?

Also consider *scripture* as a resource. Certainly you can misuse scripture, too, when helping people. Frequently caregivers have hidden behind scripture, quoting verses when they couldn't stand silence, and quoting them out of context even then. It would be better perhaps not to employ scripture at all than to use it woodenly or improperly. Yet when you use scripture properly, it can assure "helpees" that God's Word through the ages is a healing word of hope for them too. Previously we saw scripture misused so often that we stopped using it altogether. That was a grievous mistake, for it is still our indispensable guide for faith and practice.

Remember also the power of the *worshiping community*. When God's people worship together, they symbolize a fellowship that the world can neither give nor take away. How powerful the word of God is when faithfully read and proclaimed from the pulpit, or when it is effectively enacted at baptismal font or pool, and also at the table. We are not believers who live in splendid isolation from one another; we belong to a community of people who hear the Word proclaimed *together*, who eat and drink *together*. Thus, the church at worship is a resource that caregivers need to offer unapologetically to persons needing help.

Finally, remember that you as a caregiver are an ambassador of Christ. To be sure, you are not Christ; yet you are an ambassador of Christ. God makes God's appeal through you. As you accept a grieving wife who has just lost her husband, Christ is working in and through you. As you listen to a penitent man who has been unfaithful to his wife, Christ is functioning in and through you, offering acceptance, extending forgiveness, presenting love. Yes, you tremble when you realize that you are Christ's ambassador, but you do not tremble as one who is alone. Instead, you tremble as one whom Christ also accepts, forgives, and loves. His strength is your constant support as you minister in his name.

When Pastor Justin concluded this series of training sessions, the board did not respond exactly as he had expected. All members agreed they had a *role* in caregiving, yet they also saw that they did not all have a *gift* for caregiving. Even those with a gift for helping others realized that they would have to practice, reflect, and pray to develop their gifts. So they decided to form a pastoral care team composed of both gifted board members and members of the congregation at large who had particular caregiving gifts.

During the past year, members of the Redeemer board had concentrated on deepening fellowship as their first priority. Their fellowship had grown tremendously as they sought to grow in grace and to work together as a team. Their caregiving training also had increased their fellowship. Now it was time for them to apply what they had learned by caring for their own congregation and to meet community needs as well. Part Two of this book deals with how they applied their new skills by doing the gospel: serving.

Part Two
REVITALIZING SERVICE

Service: Doing the Gospel

Practicing the New Reality

That we are called to serve, no serious reader of scripture can deny. Literally hundreds of texts in both testaments sound a clear call to help the poor, needy, and oppressed. "For the needy shall not always be forgotten," cries the psalmist, "nor the hope of the poor perish forever" (Ps. 9:18). This is no isolated "proof text," but part and parcel of Old Testament concern for those in need.

Nor is the New Testament less clear: "If a brother or sister is naked and lacks daily food, and one of you says to them, 'Go in peace; keep warm and eat your fill,' and yet you do not supply their bodily needs, what is the good of that?" (Jas. 2:15–16). Can there be any doubt that the God revealed in scripture cares about human need and wants us to care too?

Service was the underlying reality of Jesus' life and ministry. From the beginning of his ministry to the end, he took "the form of a slave...humbled himself and became obedient to the point of death—even death on a cross" (Phil. 2:7–8). Drawing deeply on the servant songs of the Old Testament, Jesus fleshed out in word and deed what it means to be a servant. Who can forget his surprising words, "But I am among you as one who serves" (Lk. 22:27b)? And who does not remember his stunning deed of pouring water into a basin and washing his disciples' feet (Jn. 13:5)?

Indeed, Jesus was the servant par excellence, and he called us to go and do likewise. In fact, he even said, "Truly I tell you, just as you did it to one of the least of these who are members of my family, *you did it to me*" (Mt. 25:40, italics mine). Thus, when you feed the hungry, clothe the naked, visit the sick and the prisoner, and welcome the stranger, you minister to Christ himself. Does not Jesus' statement put a face on the needy—*his own face*?

The Open Door Community in Atlanta serves the least and the lost of society, particularly the homeless. A striking calendar from The Open Door that was recently mailed to supporters shows a line of needy people, some walking with canes, others pulling their tattered clothes around them to ward off the cold. In the middle of the line stands Jesus. Below the picture are his words: "I was hungry and you fed me."

CHAPTER 3

Service Inside the Body of Christ

When the Redeemer board next convened, there were new faces at the table. The new faces belonged to Lillian, Frank, Sam, and Mandy, four members of the pastoral care team who were selected from the congregation. My task was to help the board and the team get started in caring for the congregation and community. Pastor Justin made my task easier because of the excellent training he had already given the board and the pastoral care team.

"What concerns you most about caring for the congregation?" I inquired.

"The time element," said Malcolm. "I feel more equipped to do the job than ever before, but we can only do so much. We have a lot of administrative responsibilities already."

"I wonder whether people will respond to us," Susan added. "I think most of them will still want to see Pastor Justin."

"We feel even more vulnerable than you do," said newcomer Mandy. "We are not even members of the board. How will people accept us?"

"You have touched on my real concern," replied Justin. "I want members to see that the care that all of you give is real Christian care, not just a substitute for my care."

"At the same time," I offered, "there will be times when people may really want to see Justin as well. The relationship between pastor and people is a special relationship, and just because you are giving care does not mean that people will not still need Justin."

"Where do we begin?" asked Jan. "I'm ready to go!"

"I have some suggestions," I answered, "but first I think we ought to look at the nature and origin of the serving task. Then you can make some choices about where you want to start."

The Historic Call to Wait Tables: Luke 22:24–27

Service—*diakonia*—while deeply rooted in the Old Testament, receives an extraordinary emphasis in the New Testament. First comes the picture of Jesus moderating a dispute among his disciples about which one of them was the greatest. No doubt Jesus startled his disciples by showing them that in his kingdom all values would be turned upside down. In the political realm rulers are the greatest, but *not so* among disciples of Jesus. In his kingdom "the greatest among you must become like the youngest, and the leader like one who serves" (Lk. 22:26).

Jesus further pressed his teaching by asking, "For who is greater, the one who is at the table or the one who serves?" (Lk. 22:27a). Of course, as Jesus himself said, the one at table is the greatest. Everybody knows that! But then exploded his stunning reversal: "But I am among you as one who serves" (Lk. 22:27b). Think of it: Jesus came among us as a *server*, not a *sitter*. Who can comprehend a reversal of values like that? Surely it turns upside down everything that we and the disciples believe about greatness.

Yet all was not lost for Jesus' disciples. Although they received no "number one" rewards in this life, they would receive a far greater reward in the kingdom to come. In that kingdom they would eat and drink at Messiah's table! That dining pleasure, Jesus said, is reserved for those who stand by him in his trials.

The pathway to Messiah's table is always by suffering service, standing by Jesus in his trials. Not only his trials then but his trials now. The trials he endures with suffering AIDS victims, the trials he endures with the malnourished children of the world, the trials he endures with teenagers working in sweat-shops, the trials he endures with the homeless looking for shelter and food every night.

We may not sit at table now with the great of the world, but never mind. Jesus has reserved a place for us at his table when his kingdom comes. That promise is enough to encourage us on dark days when it appears that those who "lord it" over us get all the breaks.

The Historic Call to Wait Tables: Acts 4—6

For a while it seemed that the disciples—now the *apostles*—had learned their table lesson well. In fact, they and the infant Christian church were so concerned about the needy that there "was not a needy person among them" (Acts 4:34a). Why so? Because "no one claimed private ownership of any possessions, but everything they owned was held in common" (Acts 4:32). They sold their possessions and laid the proceeds at the apostles' feet. The apostles then distributed "to each as any had need" (Acts 4:35b).

The church's early experiment in eliminating private ownership of possessions was only a bright comet in the sky, a quickly passing phenomenon. Even then the practice was not mandatory, nor did it spread beyond Jerusalem. Still, this experiment stands there in scripture as a perpetual reminder that we are to serve the needy. Although we may not literally sell all our possessions and give the proceeds to the church, we can and should care deeply for those in need. That legacy remains from this story.

In Acts 5 we read the fascinating but disturbing story of real estate wheeler-dealers Ananias and Sapphira. That account immediately follows the Acts 4 story of the generous example of Barnabas, who "sold a field that belonged to him, then brought the money, and laid it at the apostles' feet" (Acts 4:37). But the story of Ananias and Sapphira contrasts sharply with that of Barnabas. In their giving did they want to appear generous and receive the acclaim of their fellow Christians as Barnabas did? Perhaps. Yet regardless of their motives, one thing is clear: Like Barnabas, they sold a piece of property. But unlike Barnabas, they kept part of the proceeds and "brought only a part and laid it at the apostles' feet" (Acts 5:2).

Already the ideal of service in the young church was being corrupted. The example of living communally, being honest with one another, telling the truth, and selling possessions and sharing the proceeds with the needy was shattered. Ananias and Sapphira blatantly trumpeted their generosity before their fellow Christians but *were cheating before God*. Outwardly they appeared to be generous; inwardly they were hypocrites. And both died as a result of their confrontation with Peter.

Is the story disturbing? Yes. But without becoming embroiled in exegetical and disciplinary questions, we can glean one illuminating truth from it. *We corrupt our service to the needy when we deceive others and are actually more interested in gaining credit for ourselves.* Such a startling reality forces us to examine every effort we make to serve the needy today. When we appear to care a lot but are only trying to impress others, is it not equally hypocritical?

Yet who among us can claim absolute purity when we examine our own motives for serving? Surely, no one. But be well assured that deceptive living and giving is a sin against God and the church. The weird and puzzling story of Ananias and Sapphira makes that conclusion inescapable. So be careful how you wait on tables!

Acts 6 brings the historic call to wait tables into sharp focus. Hellenists—Jews who either spoke Greek or adopted Greek customs—complained about the Hebrews—more conservative Jews who probably spoke Aramaic. Now the Hellenists contended that "their widows were being neglected in the daily distribution of food" (Acts 6:1). Widows who had no legal protection could become destitute, so what was the church to do? It "quickly copied the Jewish custom of providing funds for their relief."[1]

Enter the twelve apostles. "It is not right," they said, "that we should neglect the word of God in order to *wait on tables*" (Acts 6:2, italics mine). They then enjoined the whole community to select seven men "of good standing, full of the Spirit and of wisdom" (Acts 6:3a). Strangely, the apostles had not learned Jesus' table lesson very well! And equally astounding, the seven who were chosen did not restrict their serving to tables but also served the Word by boldly proclaiming the good news about Jesus. Stephen became the first Christian martyr, while Philip became a famous evangelist. The New Testament tightly links service and witness, a fact lost on the Twelve, though not on the Seven chosen here.

Thus, in Acts 4—6 we see how the call to wait tables emerged in the early church. The focus of their concern was the needy and how to help them. *Their concern began with their own community, "the whole group of those who believed"* (Acts 4:32a). And so must ours. Though the needs change from era to era—perhaps, for example, from food and clothes at one time to housing and jobs at another—the challenge to the church is mandated in the metaphor "to wait on tables." In fact, that very call might have originally meant administering the financial affairs of the church. To the Roman Christians, Paul was also saying, "Contribute to the needs of the saints" (Rom. 12:13a). The "saints" were rank-and-file members, not extraordinary persons like Francis of Assisi or Mother Teresa of Calcutta.

Selective Service

Even if the New Testament call to "wait on tables" is clear, those who "sit at the table" of human need are not. Who are the needy in our congregations? Hunger, for example, is not the problem for most American congregations that obesity is. Also, are not "widows" today eligible for Social Security? Further, are not some of the neediest in our midst those who live in fine homes and who drive luxury cars?

So four questions surface at once when we care for others:

1. What human needs exist in our congregation?
2. How do we identify the most significant needs of our own members?
3. How do we decide which needs to meet?
4. What resources do we have to enable us to meet the needs we have identified and prioritized?

And yet, even after we have answered these questions we are only half-way home. We then have to make sure we have trained people, as in a pastoral care team, to minister in the name of Christ to those who hurt. Then we have to encourage those who serve and monitor their progress. No easy problems, these, but a few suggestions will help you review the process and get started.

Assess the pastoral needs in your congregation. What are the principal needs of your family of faith? Has your board ever been intentional in answering this question? You might be surprised if you took it seriously. For example, an honest attempt to address the question might reveal more suffering, loneliness, hurt, and alienation than you ever imagined. On the surface, all may seem to be well in the lives of many members. Only when you look beneath the mask that they wear can you see persons struggling for life.

Of course, *overt* pastoral needs will never require a magnifying glass to discover, for church members everywhere suffer from debilitating illnesses like cancer and face major surgery such as triple bypass operations. They grieve the loss of a spouse or a job or a child who has grown up and moved away. They are rocked by marital discord and heartbreaking divorces. They sustain drunk-driving convictions and endure abusive relationships. They struggle with the adjustment of retirement and no longer feel as useful and needed as before. In other words, "Never morn wore to evening but some heart did break." Find out which hearts are breaking; then use all your pastoral skills to help them heal.

The Redeemer board, with the help of the pastoral care team, took immediate steps to address overt pastoral needs for which they had received training. Each of them was already in charge of a geographic district in the congregation. They agreed to contact each family in their district once a quarter to determine how things were going and to ask whether they had any prayer requests. If particular problems came to light, the board members responded. Some of them also gave reports at every meeting about their own "flocks." Quarterly reports were necessary from each district to keep in touch with families and also to demonstrate concern for the congregation in times other than the stewardship season.

In addition, each board member signed up for a month at a time for hospital and bereavement visitation as needed. In the Redeemer congregation this occasionally required considerable extra work. At other times, when all was quiet on the pastoral front, little additional ministry was required. But the board was determined to "contribute to the needs of the saints," as Paul had enjoined (Rom. 12:13a).

Conduct a needs assessment survey to help you further diagnose your situation. Elaborate data-gathering techniques abound. A good example is the *Handbook for Congregational Studies* as a starting point.[2] Also, *Needs Assessment: An Exploratory Critique* can prove useful,[3] as well as *Congregational Mission Studies.*[4] But I must warn you at this point not to collect mountains of data that will only gather dust in your church closets and discourage you. It's far better to keep it simple as you commence.

In my consulting work I have often used a simplified form—"My View of the Church"—that asks a wide sample of people in the congregation these questions:

1. In the space below, identify and affirm the strengths, assets, and distinctive resources of our church.
2. What specific needs, hurts, and hopes do our members have that we are not now addressing?
3. What are the unmet needs of people living in our community that we need to care about?
4. What world needs and issues should we be concerned about in our church?

At this point, decide whether you want to gather data about community needs while you are collecting data about members' needs. Although it broadens the scope of your work, it also saves you from having to duplicate the process later. But you may want to begin by collecting membership data only. The overt needs of smaller churches are much more obvious and more readily met, hardly needing a formal process.

The four questions cited above initiate a process that is doable and not overwhelming. Of course, it's crucial to evaluate the data against the background of such variables as gender, age, marital status, occupation, and income. The previously referenced materials contain methods of gathering the data without violating the confidentiality of respondents.

Collate and prioritize the data. After arranging the material in appropriate categories, you must now estimate the significance of the needs, hopes, and hurts that have surfaced. As discussed in chapter 1, which of the above items enable the church to be a sign, foretaste, and instrument of the kingdom of God? What are the core values of the people of God who are striving to live according to biblical mandates?

Thus, some criteria must be used to measure and rank the material, or else any church would quickly discover that it does not have the resources to do everything. Remember, people have insatiable appetites. Mere wants will always pop up in the guise of legitimate needs. But wise leaders always separate the wheat from the chaff when they see human needs arrayed before them. They use biblical criteria to make decisions about both future and present programs.

Now determine whether the needs of the persons you have identified are being met. If so, by whom? Is the pastor giving most of the official pastoral care? Do persons need other care? After all, many people receive strong, unofficial care in countless ways in every church—the prayer before Sunday school begins, the sympathetic question at coffee hour, the chitchat after choir rehearsal, the tap on the shoulder in a grocery store, as well as the strong support that results from worshiping God with church members. To be sure, church members are giving pastoral care to one another in unprogrammed ways.

Still, *unmet,* covert needs surface whenever a board asks such questions. It comes as a surprise to most boards to learn this fact. Is it because most of the time they have looked at their administrative work through nonpastoral, nonspiritual lenses? Putting on new glasses helps board members see a lot better!

When Redeemer Church board members and the pastoral care team purposefully put these questions up for discussion, lights came on at once. Immediately they saw that the church had emphasized youth ministry so much that it had ignored the needs of its senior citizens. And these persons had provided the finances and personnel for the church since its beginning. Only when the board leaders saw their omission did they take steps to reach out in love and care to their seniors.

If you discover that critical unmet needs exist, then you need to remedy the situation. I stress this because you may find that no serious needs are going unmet; therefore, you need to keep on doing what you're doing officially and unofficially. This is the right order: Assess unmet needs first before you embark on an extensive training program. Why? Because you may be training people unnecessarily. Of course, the training is helpful in many other contexts—it simply may not be necessary to the degree you have chosen. As an illustration, a church in our community has trained some ninety people to be Stephen ministers, a wonderful achievement. However, those ninety people found themselves sitting around with nothing to do! They finally disbanded. Either they were not being properly directed in their ministry, or unmet needs in the congregation and community were being met in other ways, or the church overestimated its unmet needs.

Discern the difference between needs and wants. Some churches have voracious appetites, as we have noted. We tend to justify almost anything by saying, "We *need* this and we *need* that." The truth is: We *want* this and we *want* that, but we don't *need* it. A need is "any identifiable condition which limits particular individuals or communities from realizing their full potential."[5] But we must qualify even that definition. What is my "full potential" as a human being? It might be possible for me to become a good golfer or to speak German. And yet, I have to ask myself whether taking up golf or German now is the *best* investment of my time, money, and energy. And so with the church when trying to identify needs for which to create programs: What are the most pressing needs of our church members here in this place at this time? Persons may want to build a tennis court on church property to meet their need for exercise. But is the tennis court the most feasible way to meet the need for exercise?

So, study your church context carefully. Although you may read and hear this advice ad nauseam, it nonetheless remains indispensable. Frequently, when church leaders move from one area to another they seek to transport successful church programs along with their furniture. Sometimes their strategy works, as when their previous programs were geared to meet universal human needs such as the hunger for community and the quest for meaning and purpose. But suppose the previous programs were based more on *context-specific needs,* such as a literacy program in a blue-collar church. Why replicate the program in another congregation where that need may be only slight? Yet numerous church leaders still say, "When I was in the Podunk Church, we used to..." So what, if your new context does not call for the same program? *What pressing needs is your present context calling you to meet?* That's the real question. Answering it will provide possibilities for future programs, as well as helpful data for evaluating present programs.

Redeemer Church Decides to "Serve the Gospel"

When the Redeemer Church board and the pastoral care team took up the issue of serving the gospel, Pastor Justin quickly suggested that the wider congregation should be invited to participate. The board agreed and then discussed the best way to receive information from the congregation. Some favored administering the simplified needs assessment inventory at the next family night dinner. However, a majority voted to use the new district plan of the congregation to gather the input about perceived needs, hurts, and hopes. "Not only can we enlist more people in the survey," said Al, "but we can demonstrate the value of the district groupings for the ministry of our church." (See appendixes C and D for detailed accounts of how to conduct such meetings.)

After collating the results from the district meetings, the board discussed the findings. Members had identified a number of "strengths, assets, and distinctive resources." Typical was this response: "Our church possesses a core group of caring people who love the Lord and want to serve him better." Another: "We have a shrinking building indebtedness that should soon free up financial resources to undergird ministry programs." Still another: "The harmony with which we work is a solid asset." And one more: "My Bible study group has often mentioned becoming more involved in caring for members' needs." Pastor Justin said the response indicated that the time had come for the church to be more intentional about caring for "the family of faith," as Paul had stated (Gal. 6:10).

Nor did the congregation fail to set forth a number of "specific needs, hurts, and hopes" that Redeemer Church should address. Leaping to the fore of the survey was this notation: "Some of our families desperately need help, particularly our single mothers." Then this: "We have a greater drug problem among our youth than we realize." Finally this contribution: "We have two families who have a member suffering with AIDS. What are we doing to help the AIDS patients and their families?" Three other respondents made similar comments about the AIDS problem. A Meals on Wheels program also received strong support, as did the already established food and clothing programs.

After tabulating the results, the board discussed each identified need. Instead of adopting and prioritizing various programs, they decided to initiate yet another meeting in each district. Pastor Justin said, "Perhaps we ought to mention all of the ministry areas that surfaced and ask people which one they would be willing to address. That way we will already have a nucleus from which to draw. Otherwise, we may simply be designing ministries in which no one is interested." (See appendix D.)

At first the board was sharply divided on whether to propose an AIDS ministry. Steve spoke for several members when he said, "I'm afraid for us to get mixed up in this issue. For one thing, I'm scared of the disease. Will we be exposed to the virus? For another, I don't know how I feel about the nature of the disease. Can it be God's judgment on homosexuality?"

With that question, the meeting erupted. When board members finally calmed down, Amanda said, "I'll admit that this kind of ministry would be new and strange for most of us. I too am somewhat afraid of the disease. However, I think Jesus calls us to care for those with AIDS/HIV. He helped lepers, and those with AIDS/HIV are modern-day lepers—we avoid them like a plague. And that's not right."

"It upsets me," said Malcom, "to think we are saying that the God we worship would zap people with AIDS. I read the other day that a minister in our community visited someone at Good Samaritan Hospital and told him, 'You are despicable to God. Unless you repent, you will surely endure the fires of everlasting hell!' That's not the picture of a loving God I see in the face of Jesus."

Pastor Justin, who had adopted a low profile until now, said, "I read the other day that we ought to let the people we are helping set the spiritual agenda for our caring, not those who provide the help. Perhaps our caring will give them the freedom and encouragement to speak of their most deeply felt needs and give us a chance to respond."

"Besides," added Jan, "what do we say to Frank's four-year-old HIV-positive grandson? Or to eighty-three-year-old Alberta, who contracted the HIV virus through a blood transfusion while undergoing heart surgery?"

After a thorough discussion, the board decided to add an AIDS ministry to the possible list of ministries. No one could have predicted the congregation's response to that one item. Five church members had already indicated a willingness to serve. The response was significant enough for the board to move forward with plans to set up an AIDS care team to be coordinated by the pastoral care team. They asked the local AIDS network to help train the team for their new ministry, which would include housecleaning, buying groceries, or just sitting and talking.[6] Pastor Justin also agreed to work with the team, saying, "There's much that I need to learn about this ministry also."

Redeemer board members continued to work with the results of their survey. They next worked on plans to add a ministry for single parents, another option that engendered a groundswell of support. Soon they realized that the service Redeemer Church performed *inside* the church must be closely linked with service *outside* the church. How could the congregation be concerned only with "the family of faith"? Did not Paul also say, "So then, whenever we have an opportunity, let us work for the good of all" (Gal. 6:10a). Chapter 4 takes up the outward mission thrust of the church's work.

CHAPTER 4

Service Outside the Church

The next question facing the Redeemer board was this: How can we break out of the narrow range of our pastoral concern? Now that we better care for the sick, aging, and bereaved, are we not called to "reach out and touch someone" else besides our little flock that gathers here from Sunday to Sunday to worship? Are we in danger of becoming ingrown? Can a congregation that ministers only to itself even claim to be Christian? What will we do with the needs and hurts of the community that the home meetings brought to light? With these questions in mind, I asked the Redeemer Board to evaluate their outreach ministry.

Steve, obviously eager to speak, said, "We do pretty well when we take care of our own members, but we do next to nothing for our community. And that concerns me."

"Not so fast," replied Amanda. "We have started a clothing closet and a food pantry within the past year."

"True," said Jan, "but sometimes it seems to me that we are putting a bandage on the problems around us, not addressing the root causes of human misery."

"That's because we are either afraid we'll stir up a hornet's nest," continued Al, "or we haven't found out what problems really exist. Besides, I don't think most of our members want us to get mixed up in political and economic matters."

"It's so much easier for us," Pastor Justin said, "to keep doing what we're doing, which is good but not enough. I think we all know we ought to be doing more, so let's get on with it."

The responses of the congregation elicited by the small groups at Redeemer Church indicated strong support for ministry outside the church. The board decided to appoint a study committee to research the issue, develop a theological rationale, and come up with recommendations. I agreed to help them look more closely at the biblical mandate for social ministry, to study how and why other churches serve, and also to see how they could best energize their members to participate.

The Paradox of Social Awareness

Curiously, the Christian church has great ambivalence over why and how the church should engage in social ministry. Of course, at a minimal level all Christian groups have performed basic services for the least in society. Have we not all heard the challenging words of Jesus, "Truly I tell you, just as you did it to one of the least of these who are members of my family, you did it to me" (Mt. 25:40)? Yet what about other issues like why people are hungry and ill-clad or in prison?

When I began my ministry, conservative churches were vigorously opposing the involvement of moderate and liberal denominations in the civil rights movement. Yet I never saw any of the more liberal churches try to influence specifically how their members voted in various elections. (Not that some ministers did not reveal their particular preferences by what they said and did!)

Have we come full circle now? The Christian Coalition, consisting of 1.7 million members and supporters, has mobilized conservative, evangelical Christians around the nation. "Voter guides are becoming a weapon of choice by religious activists, even though there are new accusations that the guides are politically biased."[1] In fact, the Federal Election Commission has filed suit against the Christian Coalition, claiming that the guides are indeed partisan. Have conservative Christians now gone too far? Be that as it may, some denominations are now "up to their eyeballs" in issues ranging from abortion and the prayer amendment to Palestinian-Israeli relations and welfare reform. Individual churches also become more involved when public issues strike a theological or personal nerve.

The fallout from the ongoing debate has had positive as well as negative consequences. For example, it has become crystal clear that, in a free society, the church—both its conservative and liberal branches—cannot remain aloof from the public issues that constantly erupt. If the church does not shed light on such issues, it will create a dangerous vacuum that all other groups will rush to fill, and other groups may not be guided by the "mind of Christ" at all. Let's face it: Economic, social, and political controversies are shot through with moral questions that affect people for good or for ill. For the church *not* to be concerned and attempt to reflect the mind of Christ is a cop-out, pure and simple.

Although various denominations may more nearly agree now that they must be involved in social issues, they still differ on many key questions. Examples:

- How should the church influence social issues?
- Do denominations speak for individual churches?
- How much does a church's form of government influence how seriously it regards denominational pronouncements on public issues?
- Should/can church boards speak out on issues in the name of the congregation?
- Should church boards refrain from making statements and merely encourage individual members to make their voices heard in the marketplace?
- Should ministers take stands on issues when they know that many members disagree with them?

How you answer the above questions individually and corporately will determine your response to the rest of this chapter.

Shaping Social Awareness

Mainline denominations hope that constituent churches will take an interest in the issues of the day. But all too often denominations have practiced what Donald E. Messer has called "resolutionary Christianity."[2] In other words, they have written endless resolutions on every conceivable issue. Sometimes their resolutions reflect careful homework, though not always. Not surprisingly, individual churches have been indifferent, if not openly hostile, to the resolutions. The community of faith, as Messer has pointed out, has not struggled with these issues "in prayer, in study groups, in sermons, or in reflective statements of theology and ethics."[3] Are there concrete ways to start shaping social awareness in a congregation?

Unearth the climate of your congregation by using the instrument on social ministry in appendix E. This instrument goes beyond the last chapter's simplified assessment of needs in the community. Thus, with your board—and congregation—use the instrument to enable members to talk about the issues involved in social ministry. The survey will help you see quickly whether members feel free to talk about their views on social issues, particularly when they feel that others disagree with them. It will also indicate how members feel about their minister taking controversial stands. It may further reveal the depth of the congregation's present involvement in reaching beyond its four walls.

Start shaping social awareness with worship. Unfortunately, we overlook how the Sunday liturgy can be a powerful means of helping congregations see the need for the church to care about community issues and people outside their walls. On Sundays a minister can pray for better Palestinian-Israeli relations or for starving children in Africa and the United States. The liturgy itself has potential for informing and reforming perspectives.

Sermons, too, have enormous possibilities for enabling people to get involved. In one of my pastorates I became deeply concerned about the issue of criminal justice. So I preached a sermon on the subject and invited members to meet with me in my study after the service if they were interested in such a ministry. In the process of greeting parishioners after the service, I temporarily forgot my invitation. As I approached my office, I noticed a crowd of people gathered in the hallway outside. I asked someone, "What are all these people doing here?" Smiling, he replied, "They came at your invitation to get involved in the issue of criminal justice!" Embarrassed but grateful nonetheless, I then met with twenty-seven people, who started a vital ministry to a nearby correctional institution that lasted for years. Surprise! Sermons still help people do what they know the church should do.

Heighten social awareness with scripture. Not only *shape* it with scripture, but *base* it on scripture. Whenever church leaders consider social ministry, they need to ground it in the Bible. But how? Not with one text chosen at random—not even the parable of the last judgment in Matthew 25—but with a more thorough study of both the Old and the New Testament. In *Social Ministry,* Dieter Hessel draws from many relevant texts from both testaments. Exploring his "Index of Scripture References" will provide grist for any study group's mill, either in terms of a survey of an entire testament or an in-depth study of one book in each testament.[4]

Finding relevant biblical material is not the problem, for a plethora of texts is available. Rather, our problem is that we don't study the whole Bible, either through fear or through outright neglect. Are we not sometimes like Mark Twain, who reportedly said, "It's not the parts of the Bible I don't understand that bother me, but the parts I do understand." Dieter Hessel, as an illustration, points out that "oppression is the subject of 300 Hebrew and Greek texts, 122 of which see oppression as the cause of poverty."[5] Granted, we are uncomfortable when we consider how modern-day oppression—economic, political, or social—also causes poverty. But does not discipleship cause us to be faithful to the whole gospel, not just part of it?

Also shape social awareness with your denominational ethos. If you are a Baptist, you will glean the importance of separating church and state. If you are a Presbyterian, you will learn about John Calvin's legacy that we should serve a sovereign God in all of life. If you are a Methodist, you will be influenced by John Wesley's concern for the poor. If you are a Quaker, you will remember John Woolman, who sparked a long campaign against slavery in America, showing the horror of oppression. So it goes from denomination to denomination, each of which contains a history not only of its theological formation but of its social formation as well. These denominational histories are often powerful "drivers" in the actions of their present-day heirs.

Moreover, lodged in all denominations are statements, written or implied, about the mission of the church. My own denomination contains a foundational statement called "The Great Ends of the Church," among which ends are "the promotion of social righteousness, and the exhibition of the Kingdom of Heaven to the world."[6] All officers of our church study such statements and subscribe to them. When they subsequently initiate social ministries, they may rely on those statements for a rationale for each ministry. In the Episcopal Church, candidates for baptism are asked, "Will you seek and serve Christ in all persons, loving your neighbor as yourself?"[7] Thus, persons are baptized into a servant ministry. To be a Christian is to serve.

Study the history of your particular church from the standpoint of its heroes and heroines, its crises down through the years, and the stories that have shaped its ethos. Carl S. Dudley and his associates surveyed forty typical congregations in Indiana and Illinois to discover where they received their vision for social ministries. They found that stories compelled the churches to act.[8]

Five different motifs characterized the stories the churches told. *Survivor* stories reflected congregations that faced overwhelming odds but were surviving. *Crusader* stories indicated that the churches had strong leaders who were willing to tackle tough problems. *Pillar* stories arose in churches whose ethos revealed either a sense of place or time or building or particular mindset—they were "pillars" of the community. *Pilgrim* stories, on the contrary, focused not on place but on the people who passed through their churches—the churches were thus ministering to a pilgrim people. *Servant* stories were told by churches where service was at the heart of what they were doing, both for people in need and during community crises.

The researchers found that churches generally explained their social ministries by beginning with their histories and attaching an addendum on theology. *But for most there was little connection between their stated faith and their action.*[9] This conclusion doesn't suggest that theology and denominational statements are unimportant, but it does highlight the significance that stories have in influencing social ministry.

The Dudley team discovered that their intervention stimulated congregations to "rediscover a rationale for social ministry within their own identity."[10] Also, whenever a congregation chose a ministry, they did so "when a community need corresponded with congregational values and concerns."[11]

Smaller churches in particular are more likely to engage in social ministry if the proposed ministry develops from something similar that they have already sponsored. Thus, such churches may tell stories of their past to shape their future, showing that the proposed ministry really grows out of who they always have been. That seems to be far less threatening than adopting an entirely new ministry.

Seize every opportunity to work with other churches in social ministries. Unfortunately, many churches do not know how to share power with others. They may work with other churches only when driven to it by a lack of facilities, financial resources, or personnel. Will we ever arrive at a time when we think of denominational and ecumenical cooperation as our first option, not our last? Now, in an era of declining resources for many churches, maybe we are being forced to change our thinking, for service in the name of Jesus bears no denominational label!

Perhaps the first time most churches willingly turn to cooperation develops around food, clothing, and emergency aid. Often ministers in a local ministerial association share stories of people who come to them for help. "My children are sick, and I need help." "I'm out of work and don't have any groceries." "I need some gas money to get me to the next town, where I know someone who can help me." Have not all pastors heard such stories? Sometimes we cynically repeat those stories, knowing that those who are requesting aid may be lying. Thus, we wonder whether they will buy alcohol if we give them money. We also wonder whether they are simply "hitting" church after church, living off the congregations in the community rather than working to earn a living.

When pastors and congregations share experiences, we often reach three conclusions. We agree first of all—explicitly or implicitly—that we are called to serve, yet we want to serve more effectively. Second, we need to be in touch with one another about who is coming to whom for help, so that we help the people who most need it and deserve it. And finally, we soon conclude that we should pool our resources to better serve the community.

Such was the development of a ministry in one community where I served as pastor. The Stone Mountain Ministerial Association started both a vital food pantry and a clothes closet. The food pantry, located in a Lutheran church, distributes food to needy church members referred by pastors of the cooperating churches. It also distributes food to needy "walk-ins," who are referred to the pantry by the Equal Opportunity Authority (EOA) or the DeKalb Family and Children's Services. Persons are given a three-day supply of food and may return twice more during the year, with exceptions being made for crucial needs.

The seventeen participating churches of the association agree to staff the pantry with two volunteers per day for three weeks during the year. They also donate financial support, plus a "food of the month."

Also of note is the involvement of other community agencies and institutions. Kroger, a major grocery store chain, continues to donate bread and other items. The Optimist Club gave a large freezer. An elementary school collected 1,700 cans of food. Scout troops and banks also participate, making the food pantry not only an interdenominational but also a total community effort.

The clothes closet, housed in the Presbyterian church across the street from the Lutheran church, is also supported by the ministerial association. Staffed by volunteers from ten of the seventeen churches, the clothes closet meets a growing need in the changing community. Instructions for using the closet have now been translated into Arabic, Somali, Slavic, and Spanish.

Church members from the participating churches or nonmembers referred by EOA, Family and Children's Services, or World Relief are allowed to select clothes up to a maximum of four outfits per family member. The closet is open three days a week. While seventeen churches support the food pantry, only ten are involved in the clothes closet. Leaders are at a loss to explain the discrepancy. Is the thought of alleviating hunger a more compelling motivator than clothing people? Still, the entire project provides an example of how churches working together can accomplish more than any church could do separately.

No one reading these pages will conclude that providing a three-day supply of groceries or another outfit will meet the needs of the poor. Much more is involved to help them claim the social benefits to which they are entitled and also to break any possible cycle of dependency. Therefore it was crucial for the helping churches to work closely with other community agencies like the EOA, World Relief, and Family and Children's Services to help them more holistically. The aid recipients often needed legal aid, job assistance, health care, and information about Social Security and food stamps.

Invariably, as churches become more familiar with the needs of the poor, members begin to change their perspective. They see how the misery of the least may be caused or exacerbated by societal, personal, institutional, and business factors over which they have little control. Duly incensed by the injustices unearthed, churches may then feel the moral urgency to protest.

Prime Time Live, for example, featured a lead story on a major car manufacturer whose money-lending business was described by many as "loan sharking," pure and simple. The lending arm of the company, it was claimed, targets low-income minority people for loans and sucks them into a bottomless pit of ever-increasing interest charges through "flipping"—refinancing old loans at higher and higher rates. When people lose their homes and come to food pantries, clothes closets, and homeless shelters for aid in the aftermath, churches need to do more than graciously pass out emergency supplies. As individuals and as churches, they can also confront companies about any predatory practices that prey on the poor.

Ah, there's where the trouble starts, the "hornet's nest" that board member Al feared unleashing on the congregation. Members of our churches may work for the very companies that prey on the poor. If a church starts poking around, it may step on some toes, maybe the toes of its own members. When their livelihood is threatened, they are naturally reluctant to become proactive. Not many people welcome such conflicts, rationalizing, "We've got enough trouble around here already without stirring up another mess!"

Health activists gathered at a recent meeting of a large tobacco company. One shareholder said she was "more interested in justice than money." But another shareholder replied, "I am more interested in profits. When I am interested in the other, I go to church."[12] No, no! *Christians do go to church to learn about justice, but then they go into the marketplace to work for it.* How long will we continue to split our worship on Sunday from our life on Monday?

But it's far easier to keep doling out emergency supplies and to forget deeper, more troubling matters. *But the church, biblically grounded, is committed to work for justice.* And justice "is the order God sets in human life for fair and honest dealing and for giving rights to those who have no power to claim rights for themselves."[13] That core belief drives us to work for fair laws, to protest oppression, to redress wrongs against individuals and groups, to deal honestly in all our affairs, and to use our power for the common good. Obviously, much more commitment, patience, and prayer are required to work for justice issues of the poor than merely to fill their grocery bags, for the God who sends us in compassion into the world also sends us "to share with Christ in establishing God's just, peaceable and loving rule in the world."[14] The church cannot act compassionately without also being concerned about the multiple causes of poverty, homelessness, and oppression. God, who has reconciled the world to himself, calls on us to be agents of reconciliation.

When we as God's agents attempt to give rights to those who lack the power to claim their own rights, we are bound to incite a reaction. When we exhort property owners to observe community housing codes, we may not win many friends. But that's never the point. God summons us to work for justice in our common life—and not just when it's safe and convenient to do so.

The above account of the food pantry and clothes closet therefore reflects the most basic level of interdenominational cooperation for social ministry. So it normally makes sense for churches to begin with a less controversial ministry rather than to address the most difficult problems. By beginning slowly, it's possible to build a base of support among members and establish a platform upon which to build later. However, community crises may not always allow churches the luxury of moving gradually into more difficult social areas—they may have to act prophetically sooner than they would prefer. The following account illustrates how one church started serving, but then encountered sticky issues that required them to become more deeply involved.

The Story of a Serving Church

Westminster Presbyterian Church is a 121-member church located in Casselberry, Florida. As seen through the eyes of one of its members, Westminster was practically "dead in the water" a few years ago.[15] Although interim ministers kept the church going, the church annually faced a budget deficit. Despite grants from the presbytery, the church's reserves were almost depleted. Both the men's group and the youth fellowship stopped meeting. Only one member had joined the church in the past year and a half. The attention of the church was focused entirely on the huge church debt. To that discouraging situation the church called a pastor.

Working with key leaders, the new pastor convinced them that they needed a focal mission. He plainly saw that their inward survival look was destroying the church.

A nursing home had just opened its doors in the community. Two church families had family members living there. When the minister suggested adopting the new nursing home as its service project, only a few key leaders were interested. Together the pastor and the leaders talked about the needs of the nursing home residents. They quickly saw persons who were all but powerless now. After leading long, active, and productive lives, they had become old, feeble, and discouraged. Many of them felt that they were a burden on society, even having to ask for help to go to the bathroom. Even then they were often told to wait because the caregiver assigned to them was too busy to help. The last thing the residents wanted to hear was "Wait!" when they needed to go. It was difficult for them to retain their dignity under such circumstances.

The leadership team from Westminster became interested enough in the pastor's proposal to talk with the nursing home social director about the residents' needs. She told them that the residents longed for a service of worship. Therefore, the Westminster team designed a service that consisted mostly of hymn singing, prayer, scripture, and a short message of about five minutes.

The hymns chosen were mostly old, familiar hymns like "Amazing Grace." Many residents could no longer see well enough to read. Some of them were unable to turn the pages of a hymnbook with their arthritic hands and fingers. So the perfect answer was for them to sing old hymns they learned as children and sang all their lives. Thus, they could participate without struggling. And that was important because life itself had become a struggle for them—a struggle even to eat, dress, and go to the bathroom.

The first few services taught the Westminster worship team many lessons in humility. Residents fell asleep (in greater numbers than in most of our services!). Some of them spoke up, loudly asking, "What did she say?" One woman even told the speaker to shut up! Another said, "We don't need no preachers!" Nursing home loudspeakers announced messages during the services. Paramedics sometimes took residents out while still doing CPR on them. And yet, from the beginning the residents were so grateful and responsive that the worship team was encouraged to continue.

Gradually the format for the services improved. Westminster members discovered which residents read lips and needed to be in the front rows—they wouldn't then ask at the top of their voices what was being said. The worship team also learned that the woman who said, "Shut up!" didn't know what else to say and that those words were just the first words she spoke. They gave her a hug, which she warmly returned with a bright smile.

The involvement of the congregation in the service is impressive. Two members go early to the nursing home to act as "ushers." They go through the halls, stopping at each room to ask whether someone wants to go to church. If so, they wheel them one by one to the day room. Other church members soon arrive to turn the chairs in the day room away from the TV into rows facing the piano. They also distribute song sheets *with one song to a page, capitalized and double-spaced.*

After the residents gather, the Westminster members assume their places, some as choir, one as pianist, and another as flautist. Still others function as page turners, back rubbers, and hand holders. As the singing continues, the Westminster members who are not musically gifted circulate among the residents, touching, loving, caring, singing to the best of their ability, and just being. To some of the residents, who are touched only when they are assisted with their bodily functions, a touch of love is significant.

The ministry of Westminster Church to the nursing home is far more extensive than yet indicated. The church sends someone to make personal visits in the home a half day a week. A musician gives an organ concert every week, playing all the old songs from 1910 to the 1940s. Another member leads a weekly Bible study. The "therapy dog" from the congregation visits as often as possible!

Moreover, Westminster Church children are highly active at the home. The children's chorus performs periodically. A few of them even sing with the adult choir at the services. All the children are encouraged to attend the services and to sing, talk, bring gifts, and give hugs. When the pastor asked the children during a children's sermon how many had been to the nursing home, every child raised a hand. After the children staged a drama at the church, they decided to perform it at the nursing home as well.

The adult Westminster choir visits at least once a year, going through the halls singing. The women's group sends residents birthday cards. The men's group, recently reactivated, gave them bird feeders. Other members regularly call the church office to say they have magazines to donate or shawls and lap rugs they have made as gifts for the residents.

A rumor circulated throughout the community that the nursing home was no longer getting the high ratings on patient care that it initially received. The church investigated the report and confronted the officials with details of what they had discovered. The church's outstanding service to the home earned it an immediate hearing with the officials. The officials heard their concerns and have since improved patient care. Thus, the church engaged in advocacy as well as service.

The ministry of Westminster Church has transformed the nursing home, but it has transformed Westminster also. Out of 121 members, 61 have participated at least once and many of them go back week after week. Almost everyone who goes for the first time returns for other services. Each week at least 12 to 15 church members are present to help a gathering of 25 to 45 nursing home residents out of a census of about 80.

Note other significant changes also. A dispirited, inward-looking church with no social ministry has become an energized, growing congregation. Twenty-one new members have joined the church. The men's group and the youth fellowship are active again. Members are attempting to locate families that need help at Thanksgiving and Christmas. Also, the Sunday school is making gifts for the nursing home residents. Members are experiencing God's love by sharing God's love with senior citizens who are often powerless and forgotten. In the spirit of Jesus, they have learned not to be served but to serve.

The board at Redeemer Church heard the good news about the social ministry of Westminster Presbyterian Church. Seeking not to replicate that ministry or any other, they proceeded to investigate the results of their home meetings about specific community needs. They soon discovered that affordable, low-cost housing appeared to be a critical need for some of their citizens.

Earlier the board had studied the importance of history-giving and storytelling in their work. Members knew that research indicates that both work better when they are integrated naturally into agenda issues as they come up, *not* when they are artificially imposed on the board. So here was a golden opportunity for Redeemer Church to test Charles Olsen's model for such integration.[16] Pursuing this five-step process provided the matrix for blending storytelling and history-giving with the biblical story. As well, it led Redeemer Church to create a dynamic program that met a real need in the community. This is how they applied the model:

Step 1: Identify a significant issue for consideration. The need for affordable, low-cost housing was clearly a significant issue.

Step 2: Look at the many sides of the issue and how it "comes close" to the lives of each board member. Several members shared how persons whom they knew were trapped in inadequate housing and saw no way to extricate themselves from their predicament without community help.

Step 3: Select a scripture passage that may or may not be related to the issue. The parable of the great judgment in Matthew 25:31–46 speaks generally to human needs of this type.

Step 4: Ask yourselves three questions. (1) What does the text say? (2) What does the story mean? (3) What would it be in me/us?[17] Studying Matthew 25 provided ample material for motivating the Redeemer board to tackle the issue of affordable housing, as well as a host of other problems. They realized that Jesus might just as easily have said, "I was homeless, and you gave me shelter," as to have said, "I was naked and you gave me clothing" (Mt. 25:36).

Step 5: Returning to the issue under consideration, can you identify any new "twists" or insights? As board members reflected further on the issue of housing, they saw that numerous issues were related to the housing deficit, including unemployment and poor schools. For the moment, however, they decided to focus only on housing. Led by an energetic team of members, they are now working with Habitat for Humanity to build two homes every year. Slowly the whole congregation is becoming involved with and excited about what is happening.

Thus, doing the gospel at Redeemer Church has become an outgrowth of being the gospel, for members are extending the love and acceptance of their fellowship to the world beyond. They have discovered that *being* the gospel leads to *doing* it. Yet does it not also lead to *telling* the gospel? The next chapter discusses this function in the life of every church.

Part Three

REVITALIZING PROCLAMATION

Proclamation: Telling the Gospel

Proclaiming the New Reality

How does the church tell the gospel? Certainly many of us heard the gospel as people of faith personally told us about the life they had found in Jesus Christ. We have also heard the gospel read and proclaimed from the pulpit and taught in a host of settings. For the purposes of this book we look only at the preaching and teaching forms of telling the gospel.

What is the purpose of preaching and teaching? It is to lead people to faith in Jesus Christ and also to increase their faith. Neither preaching nor teaching, of course, can *cause* people to have faith. Only *God* can lead people to trust God, to have confidence in God's steadfast love and constant forgiveness. Yet both preaching and teaching can create an environment where faith can come to life in a person's heart and where it can continue to grow. And where do persons of much faith and little faith hear about such a loving God? Most often on Sunday mornings, when a loving, faithful God is proclaimed and taught in sanctuaries and classrooms around the world. So how can the church preach and teach more effectively? That is now our task. But we must first see how these two important functions are interrelated.

I cut my theological teeth on C. H. Dodd's distinction between *kerygma*—proclamation—and *didache*—teaching. Dodd maintained that the apostles, preaching to *those without faith,* proclaimed Jesus as one who fulfilled Old Testament prophecy, whose life and death contained saving significance, and who would come again to judge the world. On the other hand, Dodd contended that teaching focused on *those who had faith* and was designed to give them ethical instruction and exhortation.[1]

Many scholars now argue, however, that no such neat distinction can be made between preaching and teaching. Only when the church began to organize itself after the passing of the apostles, says Richard Osmer, did those functions and roles become clearer.[2] Then, in the midst of diverse teachings and practices, it became imperative for the church to determine its normative beliefs and practices and to teach them. But in the beginning, it was almost impossible to distinguish between preaching and teaching.

When Jesus taught, for example, his audience obviously included not just persons of faith but anyone who wanted to listen. Moreover, Jesus taught about more than the ethical life, for he explained the meaning of his forthcoming death, as well as the nature of the kingdom of God.[3]

Likewise, it's difficult to find any clear distinction between preaching and teaching in Paul's ministry. Indeed, at the end of Acts, we read that Paul lived in Rome "two whole years at his own expense and welcomed all who came to him" (Acts 28:30). Presumably, some of those who came to him were without faith. What did Paul do when they came to him? He spent his time "proclaiming the kingdom of God and teaching about the Lord Jesus Christ with all boldness and without hindrance" (Acts 28:31). Once again, from these verses we find it hard to draw a sharp line line between preaching and teaching—they are interrelated. Yet each function deserves the attention we now give it, beginning with teaching.

CHAPTER 5

Nurture: Growing in the New Reality

As the Redeemer board gathered for yet another meeting to reflect on their life together, I was apprehensive. Since Sunday school attendance was down and the Christian education committee was discouraged, I was not optimistic about what we could accomplish in a two-hour session.

"Tell me how you feel about Christian education in your church," I began.

"Well," said Susan, "you asked at a bad time! I've been trying to recruit teachers for our summer vacation Bible school, and I'm having a terrible time. Either people are too busy or they will be on vacation. Maybe we should scrap our plans altogether."

"My problem is similar," added Malcolm. "I've been chairing the Christian education committee this past year, and we have barely been able to staff our Sunday school. We have many hard-working teachers who gladly give their time, but it's quite a job keeping the program in place."

"I'm glad we're addressing this topic," said Pastor Justin. "Perhaps this is the perfect time for us to step back and look holistically at education in our church."

"As we do so," I replied, "let me define some terms. When I talk about education, I mean more than teaching. Teaching involves helping people understand the Christian faith in a particular setting. Education, on the other hand, is broader and also includes administration, publishing, research, and everything else we do to communicate the faith."

The Trouble with Christian Education Today

Almost everywhere I travel the story is the same: Churches are struggling with Christian education. Sunday school attendance is often down, and educators are discouraged about their effectiveness in broadening the congregation's understanding of the task. There seem to be at least two reasons for this. First, as C. Ellis Nelson has made clear, we are attempting to educate in an increasingly secular American culture.[1] Church publications are full of stories about how mainline denominations are losing their numbers and influence in a postmodern, post-Constantinian society that is more and more unresponsive, if not antagonistic, toward the church. Gone are the days when Protestants in particular influenced even the public schools, in spite of our traditional separation of church and state.

And, as Nelson says, many mainliners have developed what he calls "lay liberalism."[2] In other words, numerous lay members no longer hold conventional Christian beliefs. Their beliefs seem to stand for little more than what society stands for. Even current best-selling books try to create a "user-friendly" God who never exercises justice, but who is always around to do our bidding. Yet belief—orthodox Christian belief—is the "single best predictor of church participation," according to researchers Benton Johnson, Dean Hoge, and Donald Luidens.[3] If we no longer passionately believe much of anything, then we have little motivation to teach—or learn—because what we believe is being taught elsewhere throughout society. Certainly we will not give sacrificially of our time and energy to teach people our watered-down faith. *Solid Christian beliefs still make a difference.*

Then, too, our faith has become more and more compartmentalized, only a private matter in a culture that prizes individualism. We open our religious compartment on Sunday, our job compartment on Monday, and our home and community compartments whenever. Our faith is not a dynamic center of power that decisively affects everything we do from home to workplace to grocery store. It's simply a private affair that has little influence on everyday life.

Secondly, we have primarily located Christian education in the Sunday school.[4] What worked well into the twentieth century no longer works. Again, Nelson says that Protestantism once permeated the nation's social life. The church was the dominant institution in the community, and ministers were often the best-educated persons, and the home also assumed responsibility for teaching the faith.[5] Under those circumstances, it worked well to locate Christian education in the Sunday school. In our secularized culture today, however, none of the above factors is true. Thus, the Sunday school itself cannot bear the entire weight of the congregation's teaching responsibility. Does not our present context require intentional, sustained study and radical rethinking about Christian education?

The Good News about Christian Education

Rethinking Christian education affords us an unparalleled opportunity to seize the day. "The church must teach or die," James Smart once said.[6] Because the very survival of the Christian faith is at stake, we now hear a loud and clear wake-up call. Smart's statement takes on an urgency we have not experienced before, because we clearly see that the Sunday school is not up to the task of being sole educator for the congregation. As thoughtful Christians throughout North America rethink their educational responsibility, certain ideas stand out like lighthouses to guide us into the twenty-first century.

In his excellent work *A Teachable Spirit,* Richard Osmer highlights "*the three centers of the teaching office.*"[7] For our study, the most important center is the *congregation,* which offers practical theological reflection and lay education. Yet any holistic picture must also include, Osmer says, professional theologians in seminaries and universities, as well as representative leaders and bodies of the denomination as a whole. All three are interrelated, and each makes a distinctive contribution to the overall task. The three centers together (1) determine the church's normative beliefs and practices, (2) reinterpret the church's beliefs and practices in shifting historical and cultural contexts, and (3) create and sustain the institutions, processes, and curricula by which the church can teach its beliefs and practices.[8] We now zoom in on the role of the congregation in the teaching office.

The congregation as a whole teaches. Not merely the Sunday school, not just the youth fellowship, not only parents, but the congregation teaches in every aspect of its life. "The congregation does not have a Christian education program; it is one."[9] That may be an old adage, but we are rediscovering its aptness today.

Certainly the central occasion for Christian education is *public worship on the Lord's Day.* Then we hear the word of God both read and proclaimed. The hymns powerfully convey the truth of God. The prayers help us talk to and listen to God. The sacraments enact and "seal" the Word. How can we accurately estimate the power of public worship to shape our beliefs and Christian lifestyle? Although the character of Sunday has changed for many, it still is the primary occasion for Christian nurture.

The *structures* of the congregation also teach more than we realize. Whom we choose to lead us in the church and how we choose them is significant. Do we select only longtime members? adults? men? But what about women and youth? Our selection processes teach members what and whom we value. Children, for example, quickly learn what adults think of them. This truth came home to me forcefully when I was once preaching in a small church. Later I was asked to return thanks at the meal that followed. A nine-year-old girl asked me whether she could ask the blessing. As we stood in a circle holding hands and listening to her heartfelt prayer, I was struck by what her congregation had taught her. She was accepted, valued, and encouraged in a way that many children—and adults—never know! Is that not a crucial part of Christian nurture?

The *mission activities* of the church further demonstrate and teach the Christian faith. Building houses for Habitat for Humanity or Agape, Inc., or constructing churches and Sunday school rooms in Mexico, the Caribbean, and Central America also dramatically teach the faith. As Tex Sample has said, "Habitat for Humanity is a significant program because its mission clearly has a theological and faith purpose and meaning, and because for a good many, participation involves learning on the job. So much of our work in the church involves teaching people *about* the faith and *then* asking how this can be implemented."[10]

When church members, staffs, and youth complete such learning on the job, they often say they received far more than they gave. They learn by doing, by serving. They put their faith into action. They depend on one another for help. They wrestle with faith issues. Together they discover God's will and experience God's presence among them. Several times I have seen groups of adults and youth return from service projects more energized and convinced of the power of the gospel than ever before. Serving teaches.

So we cannot rigidly separate Christian education from social ministry. Are they not vitally interconnected? One of my grandsons spends a week each summer with other youth and adults at a rustic campsite, helping the needy and elderly in that community. Each day they go out to repair and paint homes, rake yards, and extend a listening ear to those in trouble. Although primarily social ministry, their service is intensely educational nonetheless.

The congregation also teaches through its *informal conversation and unstructured life.* Charles R. Foster has stressed the importance of what he calls "curricular undercurrents" in educating people in the church.[11]

Prominent among such undercurrents is the informal conversation of every congregation. Informal conversation takes place among church members, before, during, and after church events. It ripples through hallways and spills over to the softball field. It questions, it probes, it jokes, it emotes, and, yes, it gossips.

Foster divides these informal conversations into three categories: thinking, belonging, and creating. In other words, informal conversation supports and enhances our thinking and learning as we explore the questions of human existence that emerge in the classroom or on a pastoral visit. By telling stories, informal conversation also enables members to feel that they belong not only to their particular church but to the historic faith as well. Congregational chitchat further helps members solve problems or explore new possibilities as they prepare the elements for the Lord's supper or gather after a Sunday service to talk about the latest breakdown of the air conditioner.

Informal conversation goes on so routinely that we hardly notice it. When Sunday school is over, participants may keep talking, evaluating, and asking additional questions. When a sermon has been preached, the minister may spend hours further discussing the sermon with parishioners during the week. When a board meeting ends, church leaders may linger and heatedly discuss their actions. When a staff meeting concludes, team members may engage in even more conversation during a coffee break. *Christian education takes place in all such settings, though they are informal and unstructured.* Why not recognize the educational potential of these occasions, build church facilities that maximize fellowship and interaction, and deliberately encourage people to talk?

While considering how the congregation teaches, we dare not overlook the *home* as an educational agent. Christian parents are the first and foremost teachers of the faith. I am almost embarrassed to reiterate that we construct the foundations of faith for our children as we hold them lovingly, respond to them forgivingly, listen to their emerging questions acceptingly, and talk to them fervently about a God who will never let them go. Basic trust, Erik Erikson maintained, develops in infancy and depends on the quality of care given the child, particularly by the mother.[12] He further stated that "Trust born of care is, in fact, the touchstone of the *actuality* of a given religion."[13] "How firm a foundation," then, is early trust for faith that follows!

Ellis Nelson points out that the faith of children develops even more by the age of three. By then "children have a mental conception of God they can describe, and a disposition to care or not to care for other persons. By the age of six, children are well on their way to an understanding of God's role in life and a rather clear code of behavior."[14] If Erikson and Nelson are on target, it behooves the church to respond appropriately by helping parents become better parents, *Christian* parents.

Parents desperately need help. Persons ranging from radio talk show host Dr. Laura Schlessinger to TV personality Oprah Winfrey document every day the fact that families are in trouble. Persons are struggling as never before, trying to blend families, control expenses in a consumer-oriented society, raise children as single parents, and live without a clear sense of the meaning and purpose of life. As a result, we often teach children more about the right clothes to wear than the right way to live. We may teach them more about how to make money than how to make sense out of life. We teach them more about rooting for the right sports teams than about the "Greatest Story Ever Told." We teach them more about having fun in the sun than about serving the least among us.

While many people seem to know that parents build a firm foundation for their children's future faith, the church does far too little to help parents become more effective teachers. Any church desiring to make an important contribution to Christian education would be wise to stress the needs of families.

Of course, the *traditional educational activities* of the church, typified by the Sunday school, youth fellowships, and retreats, still teach the faith. An emphasis on the teaching role of the congregation as a whole should never obscure the value of the traditional ways we teach. I fear that we now find the Sunday school more burdensome than helpful. While we may hope that others will plan it and keep it going, we are reluctant as adults to commit ourselves to the task. As Gay Mothershed has said, "Each adult should be offered the opportunity, challenged and expected to become involved in vital adult ministry where faith is shared, where horizons are expanded, where biblical study becomes meaningful, personal and purposeful."[15]

Even now the faces of some of my Sunday school teachers flash through my mind. I can also "play back" the meetings of the youth fellowship on Sunday evenings. Surely we do not now need to abandon the Sunday school but rather to strengthen it. All we need to abandon is the unrealistic expectation that the Sunday school can carry out the church's educational responsibility by itself.

I can further ponder the tremendous effect that summer youth conferences had on my life. In fact, when I consider the influence of those conferences, I know I would not now be writing about Christian education *without* their impact. The mentors who guided me and the youth with whom I worked demonstrated the reality of the Christian faith when I needed to see it modeled at a crucial stage in my faith development. Many acquaintances from that era have shared similar observations with me.

Some Personal Reflections about Christian Education

For twenty-two years I was primarily a learner in various schools. Then as a pastor I was a teacher, as well as preacher, in five churches. Next, I was primarily a teacher in a theological seminary for sixteen years. Now in semi-retirement, I still teach occasional courses and seminars. In sorting out my own teaching-learning process, I have asked myself how I became a Christian and also how I taught the faith. Some definite conclusions have emerged.

First, the images of *people*—Christian people—dominated my memories. Said Abraham J. Heschel, "What we need more than anything else is not textbooks but text-people. It is the personality of the teacher which is the text that pupils read; the text they will never forget."[16] In no way do I intend to denigrate the importance of the biblical text as the primary standard and resource for our nurture. Yet the reality of the biblical story came alive for me when I met people whose personal stories were molded by the Story. What they *taught*, they *were* in their inmost being. They demonstrated love. They granted forgiveness. They believed for me in the midst of my doubt. They even encouraged me to doubt when I was too sure in my beliefs. And, of course, they taught, explained, discussed, questioned, and shared the content of the faith.

Herbert Ellis was one of my high school teachers. I'll never forget the twinkle in his eye, the liveliness of his rejoinders, the caring he showed each one of us. One day he taught me a valuable lesson about the Christian faith in a public school classroom! While talking with him about one of my theological puzzles, I casually remarked, "But I guess I shouldn't question those things." To which he replied, "My dear Robert, God gave you a questioner and he intends for you to use it." In an instant I was freed up to face my doubts, to probe, to be honest. I could do so because Herbert Ellis had already established his credibility as a trustworthy, caring Christian.

The teacher-student relationship in Christian education will always require mature teachers at every level. It's not just true in the home; it's also true, preeminently true, in our theological seminaries. Donald W. Shriver, Jr., then president of Union Theological Seminary in New York, recounts what a student there once said to the faculty in 1964:

> All of us have very personal questions which must be answered, and are anxiously wrestling with our faith (or lack of it). This is largely the basis of our unrest. This restlessness cannot be solved by rearranging schedules and revision of the order in which we study Niebuhr, Tillich, and von Rad. Rather, I want simply (and profoundly) to know (all logical proofs and problems aside) why

> the men who are teaching me have decided to give their life to this! And this I *must* know if I am to remain in seminary.[17]

When I told this story in a seminary class one day, a student asked, "All right, tell us why *you* have given your life to ministry." I don't remember my exact reply, but I answered the question from my heart. Although no one has since told me that my answer was a life-changing experience, I sensed in that moment an attentiveness by the students that I have seldom known! The syllabus waited until I dealt honestly with that question. In the final analysis, we become Christians through the personality and example of persons who know the faith in their own lives. Ideally, we hope that the process begins with Christian parents and continues with other significant persons along the way—Sunday school teachers, church leaders and members, ministers, as well as other Christians.

The *quality* of the teacher-student relationship is always important. Several ingredients of a good relationship stand out for me. The "teacher" must always be a "learner." Unfortunately, teachers too often feel that they alone must impart the faith. Thus, they are threatened when they don't know the "right" answers, or when students appear to know more than they. How tragic not to realize that we may teach far more through our humility, our vulnerability, and our common search for truth. In spite of all the other mistakes I have made as a teacher, I can honestly say that very few times have I ever left a class I taught without reflecting on something I, too, learned. Often I have learned that I failed to teach well! At any rate, the educational process must be mutual, or it will inevitably be flawed.

Another conclusion that has emerged for me is *the importance of helping the congregation become a learning community.* If the congregation as a whole teaches, then the congregation as a whole must learn how to teach by becoming a learning community. The Center for Parish Development in Chicago has stressed this approach. Is not the congregation a system too, along with all our other systems and subsystems in society? As a system, the congregation is subject to the same dynamics as all other systems. Congregations are not collections of separate Sunday schools, service projects, and potluck dinners that can live apart from one another. Rather, each is part of the whole church, and each is affected by what all the other parts of the church do. All are interrelated and interdependent. So as Paul Dietterich has said, "Any change process that affects only one part of the system will have a limited effect… In contrast, research shows that when the entire system—or at the very least, teams of persons—engages together in a learning process, a very high percentage of what is learned is applied, assimilated, and integrated into the congregation."[18]

Countless education events have convinced me that Dietterich is right. When I alone have engaged in continuing education, I have seldom been able to introduce new ways of thinking and acting in a church. Working piecemeal with churches does not usually work as well as working to change the church as a whole. Changes in the Christian education program, for example, are not as likely to last if worship, service, and fellowship activities are not also changed. *Unchanged* persons and structures will modify or limit changes made elsewhere. Thus, when possible, congregations need to learn how to become a learning community by refocusing their vision, reorienting their thinking, and redesigning their organizations.[19]

Admittedly, this model works best in "rational" congregations that emphasize critical thinking. When I was a pastor, I once used a similar model in a large church and found it to be very helpful. If churches are of the character and size for a total change effort, rational planning models can lead participants to *stop* saying such things as, "I sense sometimes I'm like a person in front of a dike, putting my finger where it springs a leak. I can't take my finger out; it's needed there, and then comes another leak."[20] Rather, they will begin to say, "Now we are working as a team. We have developed a common vision of God's plans for our church. More and more people share this vision and are working to achieve it by God's grace."[21]

Yet such a comprehensive process, though valuable, can be long, tedious, and unsuitable for certain congregations. Churches that are more "traditonal/oral," as Tex Sample calls them, may not find that sophisticated planning models from the business and academic world fit their character and size. Traditional/oral people can read or write—though not all can—but they appropriate and engage life more orally.[22] Their philosophers are people who tell folk stories or proverbs that express profound truth. For traditional/oral people to change will require them to use "the past to deal with the present in order to sustain communal life."[23]

In such congregations, change may more easily occur when it's simply *added on* to an already existing tradition, not when it attempts to "dismantle or reorganize or rationalize a traditional setting."[24] Rational change in a traditional/oral congregation may collapse in a mountain of paperwork and leave members discouraged.

C. Ellis Nelson suggests a more limited, but nonetheless valuable, approach that can be adapted to many church contexts. While it's a more literate approach requiring reflection and study, it's not as comprehensive and systemic as the previous model. It "adds on," yet it does encourage change in other areas of church life, notably public worship and small group life. Nelson posits—as others have also proposed—changing our Christian education strategy from the Sunday school to the congregation as the agent of nurture. In other words, congregations foster and interpret faith in God. For congregations to communicate faith in God, they should therefore consider this pattern:

1. The gospel as interpreted in a congregation shapes the lives of adults,
2. who as church officers, teachers, and group leaders identify and practice a Christian lifestyle,
3. which provides values church members may use in making decisions in the workplace and as citizens and
4. promotes an image of God that parents can communicate to their children before they attend Sunday school.[25]

Nelson's approach motivates church leaders to reflect on their understanding of the gospel. It also impels them to identify their own distinctive lifestyle that they will intentionally live out in a secular world. Thus, church leaders should look with brutal honesty at their own values, asking, "Who are we as a people?" And, "Who should we become as the people of God in this time and place?"

With candor, then, groups and classes within the church would seek to discover their mores, their values. That endeavor, as Carlyle Marney once said, "begins where we really are, and would look like this: an exposure of our folkways, an opening of our nerve ends, an understanding of our values, a confession of our fantasies."[26] This study would explore the various myths the congregation has about race, class, region, nation, economics, sex, family, and religion. Only then could any congregation comprehend the devastating effect that secular culture has already had on its understanding of the gospel and its lifestyle. Obviously no congregation could undertake this study without pain, for we figuratively scream when a sensitive nerve is touched. Yet how can any church know what it wants to teach unless it first discovers what it is already teaching by its present value system? And how can it decide what to teach unless it places its value system under the searchlight of the gospel, which calls into question every human value?

When a church has engaged in the above process, it may then be able to provide "values church members may use in making decisions in the workplace and as citizens."[27] Although painful indeed, such a study would underscore Marney's conclusion: "No renewal can come to the church that does not rise in the local parish."[28]

Thus, this approach to Christian education sees the world as the basic arena where Christians live. In the workplace, Christians are struggling with deep ethical questions about how they conduct their jobs in a context of sexual harassment, greed, double-dealing, kickbacks, bribes, and corporate spying. As citizens, Christians are fighting disillusionment and despair about the political process at local, state, and national levels, with more and more people throwing up their hands, saying, "What can we do? It's hopeless." Is it not incumbent, then, on every church to help its members work for the common good as well as to serve God in their jobs? Not to do so is clearly a frank admission by a congregation that Christianity is largely a private matter, possessing little relevance for daily life.

The gospel as interpreted by a congregation also *promotes a certain image of God*. Does the congregation trivialize God and make God simply the "god-of-my-cause," "god-of-my-understanding," "god-of-my-experience," "god-of-my-success," "god-of-my-nation," and even "god-of-my-comfort?"[29] Does the congregation "domesticate the transcendence" of God and seek to relieve members of the responsibility to wrestle with the mystery and majesty of God, whose ways are not our ways?[30] Does the congregation promote an image of a God who wants us merely to feel good or a God who wants us to trust God in life and death? As a theological bottom line, does the congregation promote a faithful, biblical image of God or an image that has been molded in our image and shaped overwhelmingly by secular culture? To answer these searching questions, a congregation must carefully study its worship and ministry.

Finally, we reach the last part of our proposed schema, which is *for parents to teach the appropriate image of God to their children before they attend Sunday school*. As earlier stated, parents begin to teach this image of God as one they can trust by the way they care for their children. Yet parents often lack the knowledge and confidence they need to address this task. Should not the church equip them with both so that they can communicate faith in God? What could be more important than to sponsor classes to help parents share the joys and sorrows of parenthood and to teach them how to teach the faith? It can also encourage them to stand firm in the faith amid the unrelenting pressures of a secular culture that keeps organizing life apart from a living God.

Yet no congregation, of course, should neglect teaching all adults and members the biblical image of God. Although it's a crucial responsibility to teach parents this image, others as well need to trust the God who is high and lifted up, yet closer to us than hands or feet. The church should teach according to the various faith stages and transitions that characterize the lives of its members.

Never should we suppose that the above approach identifies the totality of a church's mission. While it may impinge on every aspect of church life from public worship to service activities, it does not tell us how to engage in holistic, systemic change. So a congregation undertaking this approach may later want to look more comprehensively at its worship and ministry.

The Redeemer Board Redesigns Its Nurture Ministry

When the members of Redeemer Church board concluded their initial study of the preceding ideas, they went to work to determine their chief educational purpose. They saw that their overall educational responsibility was to enable persons to grow in faith and in the life of faith. To carry out their vision, they

- ***set up a nurture review committee to oversee any new design.*** They established a new committee, because they were aware that standing committees are normally more planted in the status quo and therefore reluctant to recommend far-reaching changes.
- ***charged the committee to design a format for the congregation to take a faith inventory that would enable the board to better understand the congregation's beliefs and values, as well as its image of God.*** At the same time the committee was asked to administer a brief educational inventory to determine the attitude of the congregation toward Christian education.[31]
- ***asked the committee to collate the results of the two surveys and to set up small groups to meet in members' homes to discuss the implications of the surveys and generate further input for the nurture review committee.***
- ***requested key educators in the congregation to meet with the pastor and worship committee to see how they could work together in planning public worship.*** This joint worship-education team would also evaluate the results and application of the faith inventory for worship.

It took the nurture review committee four months to conduct the surveys, collate the results, stage the home meetings, finalize its recommendations, and then meet with the board. What stunned both the committee and the board was the fuzziness of the congregation's faith commitments. They were also surprised by how few people considered Christian education to be both important and satisfying.

In light of the surveys, the board evaluated how seriously it had taken its commitment to "My Personal Rule of Life" at the beginning of its own renewal process. (See chapter 1 and appendix A.) Rather than engaging in hand-wringing over their plight, they agreed to start with themselves as leaders and their own faith commitments. How could they effectively guide the congregation into deeper faith, they asked, if they were not growing? Soon the committee made these recommendations:

1. *Offer an eight-week course each year on "Basic Christian Beliefs," to be taught by the pastor during Sunday school.* Rationale: Redeemer Church revealed a need for more clarity and depth in its understanding of God and faith issues. Regular classes would continue to meet, but members who wished to do so could attend the special course. They also decided to offer the eight-part video series *Signs of the Times: Reading Our Culture with Eyes of Faith.*[32]

2. *Provide an evening course titled "Christian Parenting."* Rationale: The church must help parents to teach their children by word and deed. The twelve-part course would use the video *Parenting for Life.*[33]

3. *Redesign the confirmation class for teenagers around the thirteen-week course called "Making Disciples: A New Approach to Confirmation."*[34] Rationale: Since the committee was convinced that most people become mature, committed Christians through apprenticeship, it favored William H. Willimon's mentoring approach. Each confirmand therefore would be paired with an adult mentor. For four months the mentor and confirmand would engage in a relational confirmation experience based on study, worship, and service. (This approach works well in both "literate" and traditional/oral congregations.)

4. *Explore the possibility of establishing a Bible computer lab on Wednesday afternoons for children, youth, and adults.* Rationale: To tap the enormous interest in computer-based learning by setting up one or two computers (new or used). The lab would teach Bible stories and offer computer quiz games—even memory work! The Sunday school could also use the lab on a rotating basis as needed. The lab could further feature new interactive Christian CD-ROMs, using such multimedia hits as *Pathways through Jerusalem.*[35] (This approach would obviously work better in more "literate" congregations.)

5. *Plan a weekday afternoon program for children and teenagers.* Rationale: A weekday program would provide another opportunity to educate the young. The committee also suggested creating an evening program instead so that adults could participate as well.

6. *Consider doing a feasibility study to determine whether to establish a neighborhood school of the arts.* Rationale: The arts are indispensable in helping individuals develop intellectually, morally, and creatively, as well as to nurture "self-esteem and respect for others and their cultures."[36]

7. *Reevaluate the program of youth ministries and expand it by including the families of youth.* Rationale: In the ever-shifting scene of youth ministries, the church must start ministries by, with, and for young people, not just to them. The church also must ensure that its youth ministries include and stress a sense of mission rather than only pizzas and pizzaz. Moreover, the church must enable its youth to become *participants,* not just *recipients,* in the total life of the church. As well, the church should embrace the families of youth in its concern.[37]

8. *Offer refreshments after the Sunday school hour near the intersection, where traffic is blocked.* Rationale: Instead of discounting informal conversation, why not encourage it? The room nearest the intersection can be used for this purpose. We can call it "Talk Central."

When the committee finished its presentation, several board members sighed, saying, "We are not a mega-church with unlimited staff, many volunteers, and huge financial resources. We could not possibly adopt all of these recommendations." But the committee persisted, contending, "We are only asking you to evaluate and adopt the recommendations that seem most needed and doable right now."

After a thorough discussion, the board adopted five proposals. Members were enthusiastic about starting the classes on Christian beliefs, reading culture, and confirmation. They also concurred that it was crucial to help parents teach the faith to their children. They further decided to enhance and validate informal conversation by arranging "Talk Central." While agreeing that the programs for youth and the Neighborhood School of Arts were good ideas, they put them on the back burner until they initiated the other programs. The idea of the computer lab took off, however, when Steve, a computer guru, volunteered to look into purchasing two used computers. He also said that he would train teachers to operate them.

With the revised nurture program under way, the Redeemer board next faced the challenge of the other component of telling the gospel: preaching. Board members would soon be surprised to learn that they and the congregation would become as involved in the preaching function of the church as they had been in teaching. The following chapter reveals the reason for their surprise.

CHAPTER 6

Renewal through Preaching the New Reality

As the board meeting of Redeemer Church began, I couldn't figure out how to initiate a dialogue about preaching. Such a dialogue was certainly needed, but would it place Pastor Justin in a vulnerable position? How could the board members talk freely when Justin might perceive the conversation as being critical of him? Thus, with fear and trembling, I asked, "What is your understanding of the nature and purpose of preaching?"

The silence that followed was awkward. Were the board members wondering what I had wondered before the meeting began? However, Al soon broke the ice, saying, "I think preaching is a message, based on the Bible, that helps us to know God's will."

"But to me personally," added Susan, "that message should concentrate on the Bible and not deal with social issues. That's where I close the blinds."

"I don't agree," said Malcolm. "Preaching has to deal with social issues sometimes. Moral questions are embedded in social issues, and I want guidance from the pulpit."

"I think we ought to have more evangelistic sermons," said Jan. "Now don't get me wrong, Justin, you are doing a good job. But I was brought up on 'preaching for a verdict.' I would even favor having an altar call!"

"You can preach about anything you want, Justin," laughed Maria, "as long as it's about twenty minutes. That's all my squirming children will allow!"

Pastor Justin, appearing more relaxed, replied, "I'm glad we're having this conversation. It gives me a chance to express what's most important to me about preaching. For one thing, I sometimes comfort the afflicted, as the old saying goes, and sometimes I afflict the comfortable. I'll admit that I would rather comfort the afflicted, but occasionally there are public issues that I think I need to address. To avoid them seems to be avoiding the gospel."

So the conversation I had feared became an honest, open discussion among board members about the nature and purpose of preaching. Contrary to what one might think, this chapter is for members of boards and congregations as well as ministers. For surely preaching can never be effective without the members' participation, encouragement, feedback, and faithful hearing of the Word proclaimed.

It's a Different World

During my lifetime I have witnessed dramatic changes in the preaching context. When I started my ministry, church attendance was at an all-time high. We were building new churches at a phenomenal rate. Many persons coming to our churches had some background in the Christian faith. A minister could refer to the prodigal son and expect worshipers to understand the reference to Jesus' parable. But no longer. Now worshipers may greet the reference with blank stares or at best with a vague familiarity of a tale heard long ago.

The mind-set of many people to whom we are preaching has also changed. Our culture does not prop up and support our faith as it once did. This is the post-Christian era in North America. Increasingly, persons of other faiths live in our communities and demand equal respect. This means, of course, that in our present sea of change more people are indifferent or hostile toward the Christian faith. The Baby Boomers came along in 1945 with their penchant for self-fulfillment, immediate and vital experience, and New Age philosophy. The Baby Busters quickly followed in 1964, bewildered by our mainline debates about theology and sexuality and largely ignorant of Niebuhr, Barth, Calvin, Wesley, and Luther. And now it's Generation Y, born after 1983, whose identity is still forming but who also desperately need the gospel. Will they react to our church services with even more audible yawns than the Baby Busters?

Clearly, *something* is causing the six mainline denominations in the U.S. to decline sharply. In 1995 those denominations "had 21.3 million members, down 25 percent from 1965."[1] Although the reasons for the decline are complex, preaching that is uninspired, unimaginative, unexciting, irrelevant, and obtuse can only contribute to the decrease.

Certainly much preaching today is ineffective. In churches I visit I sometimes become bored and start looking at my watch. When I look around, I see more restless people. Preacher after preacher talks about Jesus Christ in the dullest, most unexciting way. Sometimes they read their sermons mechanically and are so tied to their manuscripts that they would probably faint if a sudden gust of wind came along and blew their notes off the pulpit.

I have heard far too many "feel good" sermons "where seldom is heard a discouraging word," certainly not a prophetic word reflecting how sin affects the human condition and every institution in society.

How does the preacher use the Bible? Is the text an afterthought tacked on when the minister finishes preparing the sermon and says, "Now what passage can I base this sermon on?" In other words, it's a sermon in search of a text!

Again, I have sometimes asked myself, "Where is the preacher going with this sermon? There's no structure that I can discern." The sermon seemingly wanders all over the map, and when or where it will end, nobody knows.

At times I have wondered, "Where is the good news in this sermon?" I have heard none, and I need to hear often that God is trustworthy, an unending source of steadfast love and forgiveness. Only then can I say, "Thanks. I needed that."

Repeatedly I have said to myself when visiting, "Now I know why this church isn't growing. I marvel that so many people endure such boredom week after week."

On a more hopeful note, occasionally the preaching I have heard has been excellent. An obviously well-prepared and committed preacher has proclaimed the word of God clearly and spoken to *my* situation. I heard good news that day, and my heart was glad.

Changing Cultural Formations

Tex Sample has helped us to see how persons are formed in our ever-changing culture. Some people, for example, are *traditional/oral* people who think in proverbs, stories, and relationships. Others are *literate* people who think in theory, concepts, discourse, and propositions. Still others are *electronic* people who think in images, listen to sound as beat, and visualize more than they hear.[2]

Since I am college and seminary trained, I am primarily a "literate" person in background and orientation to life. That's an integral part of who I am and how I've been formed—probably you, too, or else you wouldn't be reading this book. Therefore, I am using print and reason to encourage you to "examine" our cultural context. But suppose Tex Sample is right when he claims that "about half the people in the United States are people who work primarily out of a *traditional orality*"?[3] Most traditional/oral persons can read and write—though some cannot—but they appropriate and engage life orally. In fact, Sample contends that "most churches have a clear majority of their membership who work from a traditional orality."[4]

At first I defensively resisted Sample's claim, telling myself that surely in the churches I served most of the members worked from a "literate" perspective. Were they not in tune with my more reasoned, theoretical approach to the faith? But on further reflection I sensed that I needed to become more adept at working with persons who operate from a traditional orality.

Oral cultures stress memorizing Bible verses, while I have almost abandoned the practice. They learn by apprenticeship—learning from those who model the Christian faith—just while I think we can study our way into the faith. They love to tell their personal stories, while I want them to tell me how they "feel" about something. They are immersed in concrete, life-based concerns, while I pass out a Myers-Briggs inventory or tell them about family systems theory. In short, traditional/oral people are not very interested in my "literate" approach to life! If some of the people in the congregations where I preach are like that, I will have to become more aware of their needs and their approach to life. *Not* to do so means that I will largely fail in my ministry with them, including my preaching ministry. We simply will not speak (live?) the same language.

It gets worse, however. Our culture is now exploding with *electronic* orality. We think in images, turn up the volume on our boom boxes and car radios, pop in the latest movie on our VCRs, surf the Net, and endlessly play video and computer games. Do we not listen more and more with our eyes, and even say "I read you" when we are not literally "reading" at all? As Sample shows, orality powerfully influences electronic media. The oral practice of *rap* stresses memory. *Country music* reflects proverbs and stories. Countless *TV soap operas* are based on still other stories.[5]

Frankly, I shudder at the number of times I have stopped up my ears when someone with a boom box walked by, or a TV soap came on, or when I was mystified by the volume on a passing car radio. Although that culture will never be my basic approach to life, I need to understand it far better. So now I ask, "What's going on here in our electronic culture? Do I have a clue?" If I don't, I will soon be unable to communicate with succeeding generations.

Toward Renewal of Preaching

Rethinking the role of preaching appears at the top of our renewal strategies. Whatever strategy a congregation adopts must include the board and congregation as participants, not spectators in the process. For too long we have focused our attention only on how ministers could preach "better" sermons—however we defined better—and gave little attention to the other actors in the drama.

Even so, ministers still play a key role in renewing preaching. Many ministers in my generation studied "traditional" preaching theory. For some of us it was "three points and a poem," or "three points and a dramatic closing illustration." The object of such preaching was to *persuade* the congregation to understand and accept the "truth" that we declared, truth about the meaning of the biblical text as we discerned it.

Then, too, we preachers were much impressed by *kerygmatic* preaching, as extolled by C. H. Dodd and Karl Barth. As noted earlier, Dodd believed that we should extract from the New Testament the "actual content of the gospel preached or proclaimed by the apostles."[6] That content focused on Jesus, who fulfilled Old Testament prophecy, whose life and death contained saving significance, and who will come again to judge the world. Our task as preachers was to show the relevance and truth of the kerygma. Barth added a second dimension, contending that God is the true preacher in the sermon. The preacher is a *herald* in whose proclamation of the gospel God speaks. Thus, for Barth the sermon was an *event* in which *God* speaks to the congregation.[7]

Next, preaching for some of us became *life-changing* in its intent. We attempted to create an experience every time we preached, no matter how grandiose that may seem. If we preached about love, we wanted persons to feel loved. If we preached about forgiveness, we wanted worshipers to leave church feeling forgiven. If we preached on acceptance, we wanted the congregation to feel accepted.

Lucy Rose distinguishes between kerygmatic preaching and life-changing or transformational preaching. "In transformational views of preaching," she says, "the dominant focus shifts to the human side of the encounter."[8] Although the catalyst for the sermon is still the active word of God, as in kerygmatic preaching, transformational preaching stresses how the Word affects human existence. Fred Craddock has said that "the subject matter [of preaching] is not the nature of God but the hearer's situation in the light of God."[9] While the sermon is still an encounter with God in Christ, it becomes a life-changing event or happening in which worshipers find that they have new ways of perceiving or being in the world.[10]

Yet, are we expecting too much if we intend for every sermon to be a life-changing event for the congregation? Are we placing far too heavy a burden on the preacher and the sermon? Is it at all realistic to contend that one person, speaking to a congregation, can even occasionally effect change?

Actually, I still believe that the aim of preaching is to foster an encounter with Christ. Surely, it does not happen every Sunday for *everyone*. It may not happen on a given Sunday for *anyone*. But by the grace of God I hope and pray that it will happen every Sunday for *someone*. That's my intention, because the Holy Spirit is present in the preaching event. Moreover, I know that sermons have changed me and others time and again, giving us a different perspective on an issue, making us feel more hopeful about life and death, challenging us to be more faithful disciples, and inspiring us to go about doing good. If we are sometimes changed, if ever so slightly, doesn't that justify our intention for preaching to change lives? To believe otherwise limits the work of the Holy Spirit.

Still, preaching involves another dimension that we must consider. In this book I have already applied servant or shared leadership theory to board work in chapter 1; to pastoral care also in chapter 1; and to social ministry in chapters 4 and 5.[11] However, shared leadership also has enormous implications for preaching.

John S. McClure and Lucy Rose point in the right direction, McClure with his "collaborative preaching,"[12] and Rose with her "conversational preaching."[13] Blending these approaches and adding my own viewpoint yields the following picture of collaborative preaching: *As the priesthood of all believers, both preacher and congregation gather around the word of God, eager to understand what God will say to them together.*

In collaborative preaching, no gap or separation exists between preacher and congregation. The preacher does not proclaim a clear, interpretive word that the congregation is incapable of making. Neither has all the truth. In fact, Walter Brueggemann points out that everyone interprets scripture in partisan ways and cannot do otherwise.[14] Therefore, do not *both* preacher and people need to work together to hear the Word, which stands over them? *Both* make contributions to understanding the Word based on their own experiences and insights.

So it becomes crucial for preachers to step down figuratively from the pulpit, where they stand six feet above contradiction. Not that they literally have to step down, but they should identify with the congregation as friend, colleague, fellow pilgrim. *After all, preachers and their congregations have the same need for the illuminating, judging, forgiving, and empowering word of God.*

The sermon, therefore, in collaborative preaching should reflect the experiences and insights of both pastor and people. How does a preacher become informed by the experiences and insights of the congregation? By being a pastor to and with the people in the home, at a graveside, in the hospital, and in his or her office. By discovering how members look at their life experiences in light of the text being studied. By asking them what insights the Holy Spirit is giving them about the meaning of the text. All of which means that it's impossible to be a preacher week after week without being a faithful pastor. Otherwise, I as a preacher will find myself preaching to an *imaginary* congregation. I may imagine correctly, but again I may not. Do I as a man know the life experiences of women, for example, unless I give them a chance to share their experiences? Good pastoral work always *deeply* informs good preaching. Does not collaborative preaching require actual collaboration, not just imagination?

But more specifically, how does the preacher become aware of the congregation's experiences and insights? *The presermon study or discussion group* is a useful notion. John S. McClure offers the most comprehensive model for such a study group, which he calls the "sermon roundtable."[15]

McClure's roundtable approach yields much material for sermon preparation that preachers cannot simply imagine or construct on their own. As Elisabeth Schüssler Fiorenza has contended, the preacher's experiences and articulations are never universal and normative, and they need the corrective of multiple experiences of God's people.[16] Moreover, lay participation always greatly heightens their own interest in sermons. They eagerly await a message they know they have helped to shape.

In setting up a sermon roundtable group, McClure offers advice on everything from the preacher's preparation to the time breakdown for each part of the meeting. When preachers review the actual *dynamics* of the roundtable conversation, they need not repeat verbatim what was said. Instead, they should feel free to "rephrase, reorder, and embellish particular sequences of conversation."[17]

Postsermon feedback is also helpful. Every alert pastor notes carefully what people informally say and don't say in their questions and comments after sermons. Sometimes a comment will lead a pastor to call a person later to inquire if he or she wants to talk further.

Also, a more formal, postsermon invitation can be issued to worshipers to meet with the preacher after the sermon for thirty minutes during the fellowship time. William Willimon once called this activity "Lemonade and Conversation."[18] I specifically ask for this kind of dialogue after preaching controversial sermons. One sermon in particular on the school desegregation crisis in Charlotte led me to issue a postsermon invitation. By no means did everyone agree with me, but at least each person knew I was willing to hear his or her point of view. Although it was obviously too late to incorporate their insights into the sermon just preached, there was still time to include their concerns in future sermons and prayers. Yet too often preachers prefer to be lonely prophets rather than to encourage the congregation to become a prophetic community.

Another postsermon possibility is for a small group of laypersons to meet *without* the pastor. This pattern frees the group to be more honest and keeps them from directing questions to the preacher. Reuel Howe suggests that they answer such questions as these:

- What did the preacher say to *you*?
- What difference do you think the sermon will make in your life, or was it of only passing interest?
- In what ways were you challenged or drawn to greater devotion to your areas of responsibility?
- Did style and method, language, delivery, and illustrations help or hinder the hearing of the message? Explain.
- Do you think the preacher received any assistance from the congregation in the preparation and delivery of the sermon. If so, describe; if not, why not?[19]

While there are both pros and cons regarding the preacher's presence or absence in postsermon feedback, it's essential for the preacher somehow to receive it and respond to it. At any rate, presermon groups and postsermon feedback demonstrate to members that preaching is a partnership. It's not just the minister's sermon; it's the *church's* sermon, as Howe maintained.[20]

Yet another benefit results when laypersons are invited into the preaching partnership. When preacher and people discuss their mutual experiences and insights living under the Word, they create a climate of safety and trust for *both*.[21] Members see—perhaps for the first time—that they are valued for who they are in their own uniqueness.

Equally remarkable is that a climate of safety and trust frees the preacher from feeling shackled by the opinions and expectations of the congregation, for deep in the heart of every preacher at one time or another lies an intense conviction about a particular issue or crisis. With the proper preaching climate, all preachers will more readily preach the word of God as they interpret it. I vividly remember God's message to Jeremiah, "I am now making my words in your mouth a fire"

(Jer. 5:14a). Thus, all preachers need to listen for God's message to them and not be bound by the experiences and insights of others.

Also, members are often interested in their preacher's own experiences. Particularly in more oral congregations, members want to know about their preacher's relationship to Jesus and also what he or she thinks about prayer. "Traditional/oral people," says Tex Sample, "make a sharp distinction between theories about God and 'actually knowing the Lord.'"[22] To emphasize collaborative preaching does not excuse or prohibit preachers from drawing on their own experiences. After all, as Katherine Paterson has noted, "the only raw material I have for the stories I tell lies deep within myself."[23] What's important is for preachers to add the raw material of others to their experiences and to look at both in light of the Story.

Collaborative preaching thus insists that both preachers and members have valuable experiences and insights to bring to the homiletical task. Recall also the rest of God's message to Jeremiah, "I am now making my words in your mouth a fire, and this people wood, and the fire shall devour them" (Jer. 5:14). If the word of God is that powerful, the preacher needs to be careful! Although many churches have been burned by arsonists' hate in recent years, few congregations need to be "devoured" by God's word as proclaimed by preachers. When preachers listen carefully to the insights and experiences of their members, the words of prophetic "fire" that they speak will be shaped, though not muted, by their pastoral concern for the congregation; and the congregation will more willingly hear their message because the preachers themselves will have earned the right to be heard by their own attentive listening.

In collaborative preaching the preacher's own preparation for the sermonic event is still important. Every sermon should emerge from the pulpit only after intense study and much prayer. There's no substitute for this hard work. *But laity, partners in preaching, have an equally important responsibility when the sermon is preached.* They are to participate by hearing the word faithfully. As one denominational worship guide describes it, the people are to

(a) discern Jesus Christ,
(b) receive his offered grace, and
(c) respond to his call with obedience.[24]

Also note this about the responsibility of the hearers: "Such participation depends upon the illumination of the Holy Spirit, which is to be sought earnestly in prayer. The words 'hearing' and 'heard' are not intended exclusively to mean acts of sensory perception."[25] Someone who is hearing impaired, for example, "hears" the Word differently from most worshipers, but hears nonetheless. Recall also another biblical understanding of to hear: To hear means to *obey,* hence the injunction for hearers to respond to Christ's call with obedience. Hearers are thus to embody the message and live it out in the world to which they return. Yet too many worshipers regard preaching merely as a preacher's attempt to get through to them by dazzling oratory or sheer persuasion.

Other Forms of Proclamation

Of course, the word of God is proclaimed through other media than preaching alone. We unnecessarily restrict the word of God when we confine it only to the preaching event. For surely the people of God proclaim and respond to the Word in many other ways that are also faithful to scripture.

When anthems and solos are based on scriptural texts, they proclaim the drama of grace. No one who has heard "O Holy Night" powerfully sung on Christmas Eve will likely doubt that the gospel was announced.

When cantatas and oratorios tell the biblical story, they proclaim the drama of grace. Witness the power and popularity of the "Hallelujah Chorus" of Handel's *Messiah.*

When psalms, hymns, and spirituals reflect biblical faith, they proclaim the drama of grace. The haunting strains of "Were You There When They Crucified My Lord" have lingered in our ears and hearts after many church services.

When drama, dance, and poetry, and other human art forms are true to our biblical foundations, they too proclaim the drama of grace.[26] Willow Creek Community Church in South Barrington, Illinois, effectively brings biblical passages to life through skits on its huge stage. Increasingly in other congregations one hears a preacher finish her sermon only to be followed by a dancer who beautifully interprets the text, showing a new way to "hear the Word."

Hearing and Seeing

Preachers are now giving more and more attention to the relation in communication between the *aural*—hearing—and the *visual*—seeing. That relationship may be shifting, as some observers have pointed out. College students evaluate videos more positively than sound alone. Television, with both aural *and* visual communication, communicates more effectively to them than radio. Do not today's young children tend to value the visual as much as, if not more than, the aural? While I was reading a story to one of my grandchildren, who is four years old, he went over to the TV and meticulously clicked channel after channel until he came to MTV. Astonished, I asked him why he had turned to that channel, and he said, "I like the dancing." (In all fairness to my reading ability, he did ask me to read four more stories!) Yet, for the new generation, the visual may be replacing sound alone as the locus of their generational identification. Perhaps the rock generation is giving way to a new phenomenon that will include texts from television and movies as well as a wide range of cultural imageries.[27]

So much has TV and the instant replay become part of our lives today that we hardly trust what we see with our eyes anymore. We want to check out the replay. When I attended the Atlanta Olympics and watched Michael Johnson set a new record in the 200 meter dash, the first thing I did after he blazed past the finish line was to turn and look at the giant replay screen behind me to see what I had seen. I wanted electronic reality to confirm my reality! Not surprisingly, then, some preachers are experimenting with various ways to reinforce and enhance their preaching styles. As they speak, they use a projector to flash images or the words of a biblical text or even the points of their sermons on a screen. While some would argue that such innovations border on the "gimmicky," others maintain that we indeed have begun "to listen with our eyes." To ignore this trend is to put our heads in the sand, wishing for bygone days.

Naturally, the previous suggestions about pre- and postsermon feedback work better for us "literate" people than for oral types. We like to analyze our inner feelings and thoughts. Yet feedback does not have to be cast in the form of mental and emotional examination. In more traditional/oral congregations, members may give feedback by simply telling their Christian stories and responding to sermons with their own proverbial wisdom.[28]

The Redeemer Board Looks at Preaching

Board members were stunned by the complexity and multidimensional nature of preaching. They admitted that they needed to study it much more. Although not responsible for the final content and presentation of the sermon, members saw more clearly how involved they should be both as a board and as worshipers. They concluded their discussion of preaching by listing on newsprint the main ideas they wanted to consider:

1. To request Pastor Justin to discuss the nature and purpose of preaching in an adult class for two Sundays. Justin also was asked to consider the possibility of "preaching about preaching" one Sunday in

order to give the congregation a better understanding and appreciation of its nature and purpose.

2. To explore an experimental, presermon discussion group to meet weekly with Pastor Justin for eight weeks.

3. To authorize periodic announcements in the Sunday bulletin offering suggestions to the congregation about how to participate more fully in worship, particularly in preaching. Specifically, the congregation would be encouraged to pray for the preacher, as well as to discern Jesus Christ, receive Christ's offered grace, and respond to his call for obedience. *The key point for worshipers to understand was that their participation depended on their being illumined by the Holy Spirit, which comes only through earnest prayer.*

4. To ask people to record their responses to the sermons and to place their unsigned responses in the "sermon suggestion box" at the rear of the sanctuary each Sunday. Only three questions would be posed: (1) What did this sermon say to me? (2) What lessons will I take with me for living in the world this week? (3) What would I like to say to the preacher as a result of this sermon? Justin would then read the suggestions and respond appropriately.

5. To sponsor a postsermon group for four weeks, with a different board member presiding each week. The board member would either record the session or ask someone simply to make notes of key points that would be shared with Justin. Members of the postsermon group also would report comments they were hearing from members about each sermon.

6. To put a discussion of preaching on the board agenda one year later to review the congregation's progress in becoming *partners* in proclaiming the Word.

When the board looked at all the suggestions, they realized that they could not implement them at once. Pastor Justin himself seemed to feel overwhelmed, saying, "Every suggestion is valid, but a lot of them revolve around *me*. If I were to add all of them to what I am already doing, I would not have enough time in the day. Let's phase them in gradually. I do like the idea of working with a presermon group on a trial basis, and I want to study further how communication is changing drastically in our society." The board concurred with his idea to move forward with the presermon group and to follow John McClure's roundtable approach in setting it up.[29]

Preparation. As a first step, Justin thoroughly studied the biblical material for next Sunday's sermon, based on Jesus' parable of the great judgment in Matthew 25:31–46. He used all his theological and exegetical skills in his preparation.

Hosting. When the group convened for its initial meeting, Justin served as *official* host. He welcomed them and reminded them that their task was to understand the gospel message for their lives and the congregation.

The Cohost. Jan, the cohost, coordinated the work of the sermon roundtable. After inviting members to the first session, she distributed the preaching text well in advance of the meeting.

Membership. Meeting weekly, the roundtable consisted of eight people and included men and women of varied ages, interests, and backgrounds. Jan and Justin strongly agreed that persons on the margins of congregational life were needed, not just those at the center. The board had previously decided that membership in the roundtable should change at least every four months but on a rotating basis to keep continuity.

Publicity. Jan publicized the names of the roundtable in the Sunday bulletin and encouraged the church members to give them their feedback on each Sunday's sermon.

Preaching Texts. As Jan explained to roundtable members when she recruited them, they were to read the texts in advance and to reflect on their meaning.

Group Dynamics. As cohost, Jan told the group that their task was to *brainstorm*, not *prepare* the sermon. Also, she reminded Justin, who needed little encouragement, to participate fully by sharing his insights and concerns as pastor and person.

Group Timing. The Redeemer roundtable divided its hour-and-a-half-long meeting as follows: feedback/feedforward (ten minutes); engaging the biblical text (twenty minutes); and engaging one another (sixty minutes).

Review. When the group seemed somewhat uncomfortable with the idea of recording the meeting, Justin said he would simply take notes. He added that he would review the meeting and write up his notes to include helpful feedback for sermon preparation, plus issues or problems that arose in studying the text.

After the sermon roundtable was in high gear, the Redeemer board considered other options to renew preaching. Jan, who chaired the worship committee, said, "I think our committee would like to help the congregation participate more fully. So that our pastor will not be overworked, we would like to teach two sessions on preaching for interested adults during the Sunday school hour—maybe Justin could be present to comment and answer questions for one of the sessions. And we would also take care of the Sunday announcements about how the congregation can participate. That, after all, would reinforce our commitment to shared leadership in Redeemer Church."

The board agreed to these further steps, and so began the renewal of preaching at Redeemer Church. They said that they would later consider the other suggestions, but almost as soon as they began the renewal of preaching, they saw that preaching was vitally connected with worship. They realized that they could not isolate preaching from the context of the entire Sunday service. So to worship—celebrating the gospel—we now turn.

Part Four

REVITALIZING CELEBRATION

Celebration: Rejoicing in the Gospel

We come now to the fourth and final part of this book—celebrating the gospel. Here we explore renewing both liturgy and the sacraments. This section is obviously closely linked with the section on preaching and teaching. Indeed, preaching occurs in the context of worship. We therefore consider worship immediately following preaching, because the context is still so familiar. Actually, the only reason for separating these two sections is that preaching and teaching have been tied together as primary means of telling the gospel. Of course, telling the gospel—proclaiming the Word—is at the heart of liturgy for most Protestants.

How can one even begin to write about celebrating the gospel on an ecumenical basis? Are not our services of worship so different in nature that any search for commonality will ultimately prove futile? Are not our understandings of baptism and the Lord's supper often radically different, if we observe them at all? Is not the whole question further complicated by the fact that congregations within each denomination differ so widely in size, culture, and location that it's almost impossible to meaningfully address celebration? So how can Protestants of all persuasions find enough junctions at which we can celebrate the gospel?

Undeterred by these almost insurmountable difficulties, we nonetheless plunge ahead confidently because *more unites than divides us when we celebrate the gospel.* After all, each service has a common purpose with every other service: to enable persons to worship our triune God. To that end every service basically intends to help worshipers to praise

God, to enjoy God, to obey God, and to serve God. Every service includes common elements like prayer, the Word read in scripture and proclaimed in sermon or some other form, the offering, and sometimes the sacraments. Every service employs forms, symbols, and language in time and space.

How congregations flesh out and arrange the elements of worship will vary from the structured *Book of Common Prayer* in the Episcopal Church to the "free" worship of most Baptist churches. *Where* you worship will vary from the splendor of the National Cathedral in Washington, D.C., to the cavernous auditorium of the Willow Creek Community Church of South Barrington, Illinois. *When* you worship will vary from the optional Saturday evening service at the Mount Pisgah United Methodist Church in Alpharetta, Georgia, to the Sunday morning eleven o'clock service of the Madison Avenue Presbyterian Church in New York City. Even so, despite such variations, do not all services aim to help worshipers "praise God from whom all blessings flow"?

The deep need to kneel down before the Lord our Maker lies in the heart of every person. We are unsettled and anxious until our hearts rest in God. Thus, most of us need to learn from the rest of us what worship means to all of us, and always, at the very core of our understanding of worship, is the need to celebrate the glory, power, love, forgiveness, justice, and holiness of God, however and whenever we do it.

The word "liturgy" comes from *leitourgia*, meaning "the discharge of a public office at one's own expense," and hence, meant a service or a ministry.[1] Gradually the word came to mean the services that priests performed when they offered sacrifices. This priesthood in the New Testament included all Christians—*the priesthood of all believers.* The new Christian community had no priests, for all were priests. God calls all church members to respond to God's marvelous deeds by offering themselves in service to the world, as well as in their sanctuaries. Therefore, both their ministry and their worship are part of their *leitourgia*, their total work as God's people.

So today when we worship God in a *service* of worship, we then leave to engage in further *service* to others in the world. "The early Christians," John Groenfeldt has said, "did not think of the common order of worship or liturgy as something removed from the world, but rather as one aspect of their total response to God's love made known in Christ."[2] So should we, despite our tendency to draw a rigid line between Sunday worship and Monday work.

CHAPTER 7

Worship: Renewing Liturgy

My next meeting with the Redeemer Church board followed our meeting on telling the gospel. We had agreed to look at celebrating the gospel. "How is your service of worship here at Redeemer," I began, "similar to, and different from, other services you have attended?"

"When I was growing up," stated Maria, "I was an Episcopalian. To this day I have a strong feeling that worship is at the heart of the church's life. I liked the *Book of Common Prayer* and the reverence for God it created. I sometimes wish we weren't so folksy in our worship now."

"Ah," said Al, "that's what I like best. If God is closer to us than hands or feet, shouldn't we greet one another warmly and demonstrate that where two or three of us are gathered together, God is with us? God is right here, not just out there somewhere."

"Good point, Al," replied Susan. "Yet we sometimes become so chatty with one another that I don't think about the holiness of God. We miss something when we don't help people see that when we worship, we are here to worship the Creator of the universe, who is high and lifted up."

"It's good to talk about worship tonight," added Pastor Justin. "Sometimes I am bewildered by the variety of responses we receive to our services. One person will say, 'I don't like applauding people in church.' But someone else will say, 'We applaud people everywhere else. It's natural to applaud them here too.' One person will say, 'Why don't we have guitars in our services?' But again another will say, 'It's just not church to me if we don't have organ music.' I hear similar positive and negative comments about everything else we do. It's frustrating!"

"It *is* frustrating," I said. "We'll never be able to agree 100 percent on the subject of worship. We are different persons with different needs who have come to this church from different backgrounds. But I do think we can study the subject and reach consensus on the best way for *your* church to worship God in this time and place."

Toward Settling Our Worship Wars

Our situation in worship today continues to be diverse and controversial. The "worship wars," as Marva Dawn calls them, have been breaking out among us for some time now.[1] Advocates of traditional worship square off against those who favor contemporary worship; organists line up against guitarists; and old members contend with the young. Ministers have lost their jobs fighting these battles, while parishioners have left for other churches. Many other members have become embroiled in the conflicts. However, rather than highlight all that *divides* us in worship, we start with what *unites* us.

The search for what unites us in worship, however, initially proves disappointing. Indeed, a study of worship in New Testament times begets humility in those who crave certainty, for the records of early worship in scripture as well as in church history are sparse and unclear. In the words of James F. White, "Historically, attempts to deduce norms of worship from scripture fail because the Bible was not written for such a purpose."[2] Our best option is thus to describe various patterns of worship in scripture without prescribing what must be done.

Even so, as C. C. Richardson concludes, "Christian worship in [New Testament] times found its focus in baptism, in preaching, and in the Lord's Supper, and was dominated by its faith in Jesus as the risen Messiah and the living Lord."[3] Taking over much in its worship from its Jewish background, the Christian faith both remolded and reinterpreted it. Gentile practices to a lesser extent also influenced it. It came to enjoy a rich liturgical life of public prayer, psalmody, scripture reading, instruction, and private devotions.[4]

By 150 C.E. we discover the form of service with which we are more familiar. The Sunday service—on the Lord's Day—opened with the reading of scripture, followed by the sermon. Next came the common prayers, concluded by a vigorous congregational Amen. Then congregants exchanged the kiss of peace, much the way we shake hands today, followed by an offering of bread and wine *from each person.* Early on, the rest of the communion liturgy also included the *sursum corda*—"lift up your hearts"—and the consecration prayer for the elements of bread and wine. The service reached its climax when the deacons served the communion. No benediction followed communion at that time. Here is the approximate ancient order:

Sunday Service

- Scripture reading
- Sermon
- Common prayers (concluded by a congregational Amen)
- Kiss of peace
- Offering of bread and wine from each person
- *Sursum corda* (Lift up your hearts)
- Consecration prayer
- Communion (served by the deacons)[5]

After communion, deacons took portions of the supper to those who had been absent through sickness or other reasons, and worshipers gave their offering of money to the bishop.

For almost two thousand years these historic, essential elements of worship have characterized many church services. My own denominational directory of worship outlines prayer, scripture read and proclaimed, baptism, the Lord's supper, self-offering, and relating to each other and the world as the essential elements of Christian worship.[6]

However, even here we must be honest about the various elements of worship and how we arrange them. Music, for example, has become more varied and elaborate—choirs, organs, and other musical instruments have been added. The sacraments, while still observed by most Protestants, are not crucial in worship to many. Communion may or may not be observed every Sunday. *But we still meet together on Sunday (or the Sabbath) to worship God through the risen Christ.*

Perhaps by stressing what has always been primary we will battle less vigorously over how and what to do in worship. Here we are searching more for points of agreement than disagreement.

Yet even while we stress what unites us in worship, we hasten to celebrate our diversity as well. In fact, as James F. White maintains, *"The richness of Protestant worship consists in its diversity and its consequent ability to serve a wide variety of people."*[7] If Protestants become too much alike, we will no longer be able to serve such a broad constituency. Presumably, every worship tradition appeals to certain people, or else the tradition would not have survived. While greater unity and cooperation are desirable goals, our very diversity as Protestants is more positive than we have sometimes recognized. To experience renewal in worship, we do not have to become uniform in the way we praise God. We can learn from one another, as indeed we have, without worshiping God in the same way.

The Nature and Purpose of Worship

When we gather together in our sanctuaries, what are we trying to do? Why do we assemble in the first place? As we seek to renew worship, it would help enormously if we could agree on its nature and purpose.

In Christian worship the faithful gather to praise the triune God from whom all blessings flow. It is God who calls and invites us to worship and God whom we actually worship when we gather. Is not God therefore both the *subject* and the *object* of our worship?

We come together to worship *God,* not *ourselves*. While great music thrills us and inspired preaching challenges us, we dare not forget that the choir and the preacher are there to help us praise God. They are only means to that end. Even when we applaud our children after they finish singing, we need to remember that they too are raising their young voices to God in praise. In our children's sermons we should tell them more about what *God* has done than what *they* should do.[8] God is the primary focus of our concern.

Some modern services seem to be moving in another direction. The friendly pastor steps forth and cheerfully says, "Good morning." To which the congregation dutifully replies, "Good morning." But is it my purpose as a worshiper to greet the pastor or to meet God? If you must begin this way and then make announcements, at least move quickly to give a scriptural call to worship: "O magnify the Lord with me, and let us exalt his name together" (Ps. 34:3). It is the *Lord* whom we have gathered to magnify.

In Christian worship we offer ourselves to God just as we are, warts and suffering included. We do so because we know that God will forgive us. Thus, we acknowledge who we are by confessing our sins. Is not Marva Dawn right when she says that "worship ought to kill us"?[9] Surely worship ought to kill every sin we confess, from our pride to our inhumanity to others, for only when our sin has been put to death can we walk and live in the light of Christ. In many church services, however, nothing is ever said or done that confronts us in our sin and pushes us to discover our responsibility for the world's mess. "Dr. Feel Good" often reigns supreme.

Now, I too want to feel good, but can I really feel good about myself and my involvement in society *if my sin is not forgiven?* Hardly, and the source of my forgiveness is the living God to whom I confess. If the service of worship does not enable me to expose the depths of my sinfulness to God, I will not be forgiven in the depths where I hurt and need healing, but, as we sing, "There is a balm in Gilead to heal the sin-sick soul."[10] The only balm that heals the sin-sick soul is found in the gospel that is read, proclaimed, and enacted when we worship God.

So we can affirm that worship ought to kill us as long as it kills the sin that prevents us from following Christ more fully. Yet the forgiveness of God must be proclaimed loud and clear, or else we will hear only negative messages about ourselves. Some keen observers of human nature contend that we have to hear good messages about ourselves nine times to counteract one negative message. Whether true or not, no service is complete that does not boldly announce God's forgiveness for our sin. We need to hear that good news!

In Christian worship we are equipped to serve God in the world. Is there not a rhythm between worship and ministry? "Enter to worship—depart to serve," some church bulletins read. Remember, both are the work of God's people.

So there ought to be a connection between what we do in worship on Sunday and our jobs on Monday. Can we confess the sin of racism one day and practice it the next? Can we admit that the world is too much with us one day and turn the next six into a mindless shopping spree? Can we acknowledge God's rule when we kneel in prayer and act as though sex governs our lives the rest of the week? No, the God who calls us to worship also calls us to live and serve faithfully in the world.

Yet we sometimes try to separate our worship from our life in the world. "Too often," says Theodore Jennings, "we think of worship as an escape from the harsh realities of the world, as a respite from our labors, as a sacred time and space separated from the real world."[11] But Jennings goes on to point out what a complete misunderstanding this is. On the contrary, he says: "The liturgy of the gathered community is the epitome, the model, of our lifestyle, of our way of being in the world…Far from being a separate 'religious activity,' our worship is the paradigm for a way of being in the world of politics and economics, the world of responsibility and of labor, the world of relationships."[12] What a difference it would make if we stopped dividing our lives into two parts: what we do in the world and what we do in church. No, *all of our lives, comprising our worship in church and our life in the world, is part of God's creative, redemptive, and transformative purpose for humankind.*[13]

A Model for Renewing Worship

The bottom line for church boards and congregations is to develop a liturgy that enables their congregation to worship God faithfully in their time and place. To accomplish this task, they need to take into account multiple factors, as we shall see. Moreover, they then have to strategize about how they can best institute any new patterns that arise from their study. Indeed, to work out a strategy to manage change and to communicate effectively with the congregation is as crucial as the background study itself. By no stretch of the imagination will this book posit a final solution to the worship wars that ever plague us, but it will propose a *model* for conducting a study of worship and also offer a *strategy* for effecting change. The end result, we trust, will be the possibility of renewing liturgy for the congregation as a whole.

Discuss whether you can agree that you will be guided by the Holy Spirit speaking in scripture.[14] Here we must admit that we will be *guided* by scripture, not *confined* exclusively to it. Recall James F. White's wise judgment that we cannot deduce norms for worship from scripture, because the Bible was not written for this purpose.

Although perhaps not as normative as we would like, churches should still be strongly *guided* by scripture, and we need the Spirit to guide us as we interpret scripture. See what you can learn from studying worship in passages like 1 Corinthians 14:26–33, as Paul tells the Corinthians when they come together to include a hymn, a lesson, a revelation, a tongue, a prophecy, or an interpretation.

What can you learn from Acts 2:37–47, when the early Christians "devoted themselves to the apostles' teaching and fellowship, to the breaking of bread and the prayers" (Acts 2:42)?

What does Colossians 3:12–17 teach you about music, as Paul encourages the Colossians to "sing psalms, hymns, and spiritual songs" (Col. 3:16b)?

What does Revelation 4—6 teach you when you discover that the author has cast his vision in forms derived from the liturgy? That is the only passage in the New Testament that shows us "the Christian liturgy as it developed at the end of the first century."[15]

What does 1 Corinthians 11:17–34 say about the spirit in which you should take communion at the Lord's table?

Thou shalt not neglect the Old Testament! What does Deuteronomy 6—9 teach about the importance of remembering God's mighty acts in your worship, thanking God for all that God has done, and calling God's people to faithfulness in the future?[16]

What can you learn from passages like Isaiah 6:1–8 about the holiness of God that should characterize worship? While admittedly more descriptive than prescriptive, these passages will guide you nonetheless. They will not only teach some specifics, but will also demonstrate the difficulty of finding a clear pattern of worship in the Bible.

Consider the historic experience of the church universal in worship down through the years. Although the Holy Spirit does guide us in scripture, tradition also has much to teach us. Members are often surprised to discover that what they thought had always been done, such as preaching twenty-minute sermons, is a recent innovation. In colonial America sermons sometimes lasted one or two hours!

As you look at different worship traditions, you become amazed at their different emphases. Read James F. White's *Protestant Worship: Traditions in Transition* for an excellent summary. From the Quakers you may learn the value of silence. From Roman Catholics you may learn to make the eucharist more central in your liturgy. From Baptists you may learn freedom and spontaneity. From Presbyterians you may learn to stress preaching the word of God. From the United Church of Christ you may learn how to articulate the unity of worship and social justice. From Methodists you may learn the importance of hymnody. From Lutherans you may learn how to stress baptism, so important to Luther, in all your services. From Episcopalians you may learn the value of following some fixed services in your worship.

Again, while we do not need to be uniform in what we do with other traditions, neither do we need to remain uninformed. Studying recent moves in worship by all denominations will often reveal how much we can and do learn from one another. Still, each denomination has retained its own identity in the process.

Study the tradition of your denomination. When I have taught such classes, for example, persons seem surprised to discover that in *Calvin's Liturgy of 1545*, the sermon was not at the end of the service but nearer the middle.[17] Calvin also wanted to celebrate the Lord's supper every Sunday, though that proved too radical for Genevans. John Wesley as well strongly favored a weekly observance of the Lord's supper, although his preference did not transfer to the rise of Methodism in America. Does the placement of the sermon in the liturgy and the frequency of communion make any difference in your denomination and congregation?

Also, when you investigate your own denominational history, do you have creeds, confessions, and a worship directory to guide you? Some denominations like the Lutheran Church in America do, while others do not. Are there fixed orders of worship, as is customary in the Episcopal Church, or are churches relatively free to order worship as they choose?

Explore the history of worship in your congregation. This will be very important when we consider changing worship, for change is always received better when it can be connected with a former church practice. In that way members will regard the change as part of who they are.

Our patterns of worship constantly change from generation to generation, though sometimes so slowly we hardly realize it. What we consider traditional today may actually be a recent innovation in a congregation. One Presbyterian pastor studied his church bulletins from 1939 to the present. In the 1930s there was no creed, no prayer of confession and assurance of pardon, nor was the Lord's prayer prayed.[18] Wouldn't it be easy for worshipers today in that church to conclude that their present worship, which contains the Lord's Prayer, a creed, a prayer of confession, and an assurance of pardon, is traditional? However, these elements were introduced recently in that congregation, while the simple service of the 1930s is the older version. But, to complicate matters further, today's "traditional" service is older if one goes back to Calvin's liturgy in which the Apostles' Creed, the Lord's Prayer, a prayer of confession, and absolution characterized his services.

Study the needs and circumstances of your particular congregation. Every denomination has churches that vary greatly in size, age, history, cultural background, and style. Such needs and circumstances will doubtless lead those who plan worship to make different decisions. Calvin once wrote to Somerset in England that "forms of worship ought to be accommodated to the conditions and the tastes of the people."[19] Obviously, a new church development will be more open to innovation than an established downtown first church. And will not a growing suburban church be more likely to be flexible than a historic rural church? As I visit different churches doing workshops and preaching, I am constantly astounded by the varied patterns of worship that have been tailor-made for each church's context.

Study the dynamics of change. Any change proves difficult for many people, but changes in worship really seem to inflame church members. Do it differently, and you risk conflict. How fast we become locked into systemic patterns in worship as well as in family life!

Once a minister moved to another pastorate and was conducting his first service in the new congregation. The service included the celebration of the Lord's supper. After the benediction the minister greeted his members in the narthex. He was pleased with their comments until one woman said angrily, "You didn't touch the radiator!" Then she turned and left. Stunned to the point of disbelief, the minister was at a loss to explain her strange outburst. Finally he called the previous minister to see whether he could explain the woman's anger. At once the former minister laughed and said, "Oh, yes. Let me tell you what happened. Whenever I conducted communion there, I noticed that every time I walked across that thick carpet to the table, I received a shock when I touched the communion ware. Evidently I was building up a lot of static electricity. So I began touching the radiator as I walked to the table, and that eliminated the problem. I guess she thought that touching the radiator was part of the communion liturgy!"

So church leaders are at risk when changing any element of worship, any form, any style, any item of church furniture. Lyle Schaller identifies four types of change: (1) a change in structure, (2) a change in technology, (3) a change in behavior, and (4) a change in assumptions and values.[20] The more types that are involved in proposed changes, the more complex the process becomes. The section that soon follows shows how Redeemer Church, informed by change dynamics, developed a new liturgy.

Incidentally, a study of the history of worship helps parishioners quickly see that liturgy has always been in a state of flux. Even in Roman Catholic liturgy far more changes have occurred since 1963 than in the previous four centuries![21] In this century, Roman Catholics and Protestants have borrowed many ideas from one another. Perhaps congregations will look at change with less fear when they realize how much all Christians have in fact changed in their liturgies.

Develop criteria by which music is selected for worship. I am a musical dunce! Unless I am surrounded by strong voices singing on key, I can hardly carry a tune. And yet, I love music and have always wanted the churches I serve to have strong music programs for all ages. While music alone will not build a vital church, it can help create dynamic worship services.

Through song we offer our total selves to God in prayer. Sometimes we sing *psalms* as our response to God. Sometimes we sing *hymns* and *spiritual songs*, as did the New Testament church. But always, as the people of God, we are united in common worship wherever and whenever we sing.[22]

Still, how do we judge the appropriateness of a particular piece of music for worship? Marva Dawn suggests a fourfold grid to follow when deciding:

1. Is the text theologically sound? Is it true to God's nature, conducive to the formation of character, inclusive for the whole community?

2. Does the style disrupt worship in any way? Is it honest? Does it prevent community singing or promote it? Does it have any negative associations that might preclude its use for worship?

3. How appropriate is the piece with respect to our goal to use music for the diversity of congregation members? How appropriate is it to the musical ability of the congregation and the music leaders? How appropriate is it to its function in the service and the place of the service in the church year?

4. Is this piece of music characterized by excellence and greatness to a satisfactory degree? Do other matters in the selection grid outweigh the requirements of excellence and greatness to some extent (though never entirely, for we do not want to serve God with less than our best)?[23]

Using these criteria, we may well select contemporary hymns as well as more ancient texts. We can accompany the hymns with piano, organ, flute, trumpet, or brass ensemble. The old and young among us can join in the singing, even clapping their hands and moving their feet in time with the beat. So sometimes we "can 'sing a new song' not because we are trying to appeal to the culture, but because God is present in our midst in new ways."[24]

Bear in mind, however, that creating dynamic services of worship involves far more than learning how to select music. That process includes developing a competent choir, choosing good choir directors, and remembering that, as Kennon L. Callahan has said, "Music is 40 percent of worship."[25]

A Church Changes Its Liturgy

In Redeemer Church it was the board's responsibility to oversee and approve all public worship. For some board members who came from different church backgrounds, their previous minister had made all decisions about worship. Of course, the Redeemer board shared some responsibilities with Pastor Justin, who selected both the scripture lessons to be read and the music to be sung, and preached the Word. Other matters, like selecting anthems, Justin carried out with the choir director. Justin also had joint responsibility with the board for the sequence and proportion of the elements of worship. He always worked with the worship committee to make recommendations about the services.

The Redeemer board was uncertain whether it should even think about changing its liturgy, but as members discussed the situation further, they decided to appoint a worship task force to study the situation and to make recommendations later.

The task force first agreed to offer a worship class for adults in the summer vacation Bible school for five evenings in July. After focusing on worship in New Testament times, the class looked at different patterns of worship in the history of the church, ending with a brief exploration of their own denomination and congregation.

The task force carefully monitored the questions and suggestions of the people involved in the study. During the last class a survey was given that invited persons to indicate their present responses to worship at Redeemer Church. (See appendix F.)

Next, on the basis of their study with the congregation, the task force began work on a new liturgy that would include the essentials of worship as reviewed from biblical times down to the present. A significant debate evolved over whether to recommend a traditional or a contemporary service or both. Not wanting to risk dividing the congregation into two age groups, they eventually decided to blend the two approaches. They argued that the older members needed the freshness and vigor that younger and newer members brought to worship, while the latter needed to learn from the experience and maturity of the older members. So the task force concluded that the best approach was to develop congregational appreciation for *both* styles of worship. (See appendix G for a change strategy if you decide to have two services, one contemporary and one traditional.)

When the task force presented a revised liturgy to the full board, the discussion was lively. The reaction of members proved to be a microcosm of the response the congregation as a whole made later. The spirited discussion signaled the importance of worship to people. As Jan said, "Whenever I stop and think about worship, I remember sitting with my parents and my brother at First Church when I was growing up. I don't like to think about changing my early patterns too much. I want the church to bring me stability in the midst of change." After further revision, the board decided to present the new service to the congregation on an experimental basis for six weeks.

The board members, however, first reviewed the dynamics of change. They realized that understanding the following dynamics was almost as important as understanding the nature and purpose of worship:

- *Understand that all people resist change.* You may think it's good and desirable, but change always threatens the equilibrium of your congregation.
- *Know your congregation.* Study the history of strategic changes your congregation has previously made. How have leaders effected change before? Perhaps the new proposal can be connected to an event in the church's past.
- *Plan changes with the people.* Don't surprise or impose newness on people, but involve them in the process. Ask for their input and their feedback during each step.

- *Fill the glass slowly.* If you want to fill a glass with water, you don't turn on the faucet full blast. Rather, you do it gradually; so should it be with your church.
- *Educate the congregation.* As they study the history of worship, for example, they will see that other denominations and congregations worship differently. That may lessen their resistance to new proposals.
- *Determine ways to reduce resistance to change.* Involve the opponents of change in the discussion. They need to know that you value their opinions and respect their feelings.
- *Cultivate long-standing leaders.* No change is likely to occur without the formal or informal approval of key leaders.
- *Communicate often with the congregation.* Let them know exactly what is going on as the plans progress.
- *Give people time and space in which to grow.* Plant seeds for change but don't expect them to come up overnight! People need time for ideas to germinate.
- *Seek the presence and power of the Holy Spirit.* Change is difficult for people, to be sure, but the Holy Spirit is always at work in the world. Tap this power![26]

When the Redeemer board discussed the dynamics above, e*ducation and communication* were two key words that kept emerging. "We need to educate the congregation about what we are doing and why we are doing it," said Al, "and we need to communicate with them faithfully during the entire process. They must know that we value their feelings and experiences."

While discussing change, the worship task force also remembered the four types of change that Lyle Schaller identified. Interestingly, all four were involved in the new liturgy. *Structure* was involved, because the elements of worship were arranged differently. *Technology* was being changed, because now computer-driven images were occasionally projected on a screen for hymns and sermons. People were encouraged to applaud, as when the children sang, so a different *behavior* was permitted. The services now had the unchurched person more in mind than before—a change in *assumptions and values*. No wonder the board stressed the need to proceed cautiously with the changes!

With the dynamics of change in mind, Pastor Justin announced, "Nothing is set in cement yet and won't be until we receive further input from you." He and the task force also interpreted and explained every change both in the order and the actual elements of worship.

Following the sixth service, the task force distributed an evaluation form titled "Reflections on Our New Service of Worship." (See appendix H.) Members were invited to stay for a few moments after the service to fill out the survey while the service was still fresh in their minds. A copy was also enclosed in the newsletter the next week for those who were not present the sixth Sunday.

When collating the data, the worship task force immediately saw that most evaluations were positive in tone. However, the task force took negative comments seriously. Someone wrote, "We don't like to get up and down so often!" Another person was adamant about keeping the sermon at the end of the service, saying, "I like to go home with the message of the sermon in my mind, and I find it hard to remember after all the ritual that follows." Still, most respondents liked having the sermon before the offering so that the offering could then be part of their response to the proclamation of the Word.

Other comments were:

- "The passing of the peace is an empty formality."
- "Why isn't more time given for prayer and meditation?"
- "Are we turning worship into a multimedia event and losing the reverence and awe we need in God's presence?"

The task force wisely evaluated and balanced the various responses, not allowing one isolated or vehement comment to force them automatically to change that element of worship. But when clear trends surfaced in the evaluations, they either made changes or developed a rationale for maintaining their previous practice. In the process they realized once more that no one service would ever satisfy the needs of all the people.

After recommending the revised liturgy to the board and receiving approval for it, the task force again presented and interpreted it to the congregation. Pastor Justin said, "We'll review the process again at the end of the year."

Surprisingly, music proved to be the most troublesome issue. The task force and church staff had to spend much time cultivating the church musicians! It also took six months for the congregation to understand and appreciate the fact that organ, flute, and guitar accompaniment could blend in one service. Gradually those in charge of the music program learned how to apply the criteria for selecting good music for worship. Time and again, however, various persons grumbled about the hymn selection, saying, "We don't sing enough of the old gospel hymns." But others asked, "Why don't we sing more new songs?"

Actually, the congregation was still using an old, 1957 hymnbook, and the worship task force quickly saw that the church needed a newer hymnbook. It also became tiresome to provide bulletin inserts for more recent music. They favored a change in hymnbooks when the budget could stand it.

After a normal adjustment period, the congregation responded well to the new service. Church members said worship had become much more meaningful to them. When asked why, they said they understood it better, participated more, enjoyed the new hymns, and felt more connected in their work on Monday. Does not that add up to more commitment?

Not all members were enthusiastic, of course, but most continued to worship faithfully nonetheless. They appreciated the fact that the board had consulted them frequently. It also reduced their resistance to change to see the enthusiasm of the younger members.

As the board worked to renew the regular liturgy of the Sunday service, members became aware of the importance of the sacraments in the Christian tradition. Indeed, baptism and the Lord's supper were embedded in the early rituals as worship patterns developed in the infant Christian church. Yet the celebration of the sacraments at Redeemer was more routine than meaningful. Should not a renewing church consider the sacraments also? Might not their observance be further opportunities for renewal? So on the sacraments of the church we next focus our attention.

CHAPTER 8

Renewing the Sacraments

"How important are baptism and the Lord's supper to you and to the life of this church?" I asked the Redeemer board as we continued our liturgical work.

"I don't think they are very important to the church or to me," said Amanda. "We could go without observing either for a long time before anyone would notice it."

"I have a somewhat different view," answered Malcolm. "Although I agree that the sacraments are not important to most members, they are important to me. Perhaps it was my upbringing in the Catholic Church, but I really do miss celebrating the Lord's supper more often. As for baptism, I've noticed that we seem to observe it very casually."

"I honestly don't think the sacraments make a lot of difference around here," Steve said. "I'll admit I don't really understand them. Maybe if we studied them in more detail, it would help."

"I agree," added Justin. "Only in seminary did I begin to take the sacraments seriously. My interest increased when I studied their meaning, participated in them, and reflected on my life in light of them." So began our exploration of baptism and the Lord's supper.

Our Present Confusion

Admittedly, we may be fighting a losing battle to stress sacramental renewal. In the first place, some readers may be inclined to move to the next chapter when they see the word *sacrament*. Why? Because they come from a Christian tradition that regards the Lord's supper, for example, as an *ordinance*, not a *sacrament*. Following Ulrich Zwingli and the Anabaptists of the sixteenth century, they believe "the Supper is only an ordinance—a kind of affirmation of faith that we offer to God as an indication of our obedience to Christ's order (hence the term *ordinance*), 'Do this in remembrance of me.'"[1]

Those who hold to a sacramental view of the supper, however, don't deny that Christ commanded us to "do" the supper "in remembrance of him." But they also insist that when we do it, "God offers us more than we ourselves can bring to the Supper. The sacrament is a divinely granted proclamation of the gospel, not simply a human affirmation of the gospel."[2] The supper, therefore, is a "means of grace"; it is not merely an act we do, but rather a gift that God gives us out of divine love.

But already I am getting caught up once again in one of the great Protestant debates that has raged down through the centuries ever since Luther and Zwingli met face-to-face in Marburg in 1529. Luther considered baptism and the Lord's supper to be sacraments, Zwingli ordinances. As Luther reportedly acknowledged, he and Zwingli seemed to be of a different spirit on this point; many of their followers still are. But whether you regard baptism and the Lord's supper as sacraments or ordinances, use this chapter to lead you toward renewal and deeper meaning in both.

Yet the debate over the sacraments is much broader than the sacrament-ordinance controversy. Even Christians who hold to the sacramental nature of baptism and the Lord's supper—Lutherans, Methodists, Presbyterians, Episcopalians, Roman Catholics, Orthodox, and others—disagree over many other nuances of the sacraments.

With baptism, for example, *why* do we baptize—to initiate the candidate into the Christian faith or to signify the forgiveness of sins or what? *Whom* do we baptize, children of believers as well as believers or believers only? *How* do we baptize, by sprinkling, pouring, or immersion, or does it make any difference? *What formula* do we use when we baptize, "Father, Son, and Holy Spirit," or some expression that avoids male language? *Where* do we baptize, at font or pool? *What other actions* are appropriate, such as anointing with chrism by tracing the sign of the cross on the candidate's forehead, or the laying on of hands and praying for the gift of the Holy Spirit?

Nor is the Lord's supper less complex. *What* do we mean by this service? *How* is Christ present, or is he particularly present at all? *What menu* do we use—bread and wine only, or bread and grape juice, or...pizza and Coke? *Who* serves as celebrant, clergy or lay, and if lay, who? *Who* can receive it, baptized only, confirmed only, or whosoever comes? *Which* actions are essential, four with the bread and three with the cup or a combination called the fourfold action? *Where* do we celebrate the supper, in churches or homes or retreats or all of the above? *How* do we receive it, by common cup, intinction, or individual cups? *When* do we observe it, weekly, monthly, or quarterly? *What do we even call it*, holy communion, the Lord's supper, mass, or eucharist? Bewildering, isn't it?

To further complicate matters, many of us who teach and write about sacraments today grew up in congregations that neglected the sacraments. The main memory I have about the Lord's supper was watching the elders in my "home" church carefully remove and fold a white cloth that covered the elements. I also wondered why we drank grape juice but called it "wine." And we only observed it once in a while, which I later discovered was quarterly.

Baptism was no more memorable for me. My interest always perked up when a family presented their baby for the sacrament, but I didn't understand it or even try to explain it. It was just something the minister did soon after a child was born. Oh, yes, I do remember that after he dipped his hand in the water he sometimes shook it to get the water off before touching the baby's head! So he baptized more by *touching* than by *sprinkling*! Nor do I recall seeing many adults being baptized. So it's not surprising that my view of the sacraments was hardly meaningful.

My experience with the sacraments is similar to that of numerous Christians. As they have grown in Christian maturity, they have found that the sacraments have been on the margins of their faith journey, not at the center. They cannot relate to the Anglican woman who said, "I just live for my weekly communion." Have not many Christians lived without observing communion more than once every three months, and even then without any special meaning? Thus, as James F. White has noted:

> [W]e are forced to admit that sacraments are certainly not essential to Christian worship, as the Quakers show full well. Even a moderate sacramental life seems quite acceptable to most Presbyterians and Methodists. And many Episcopalians and Lutherans seem content with the eucharist one Sunday a month. Christian worship for these groups is strong and vital but not necessarily sacramental. Jesus Christ alone remains the first and enduring sacrament, the only permanent encounter of God and humanity for all groups of Christian worshipers.[3]

So, why not accept White's statement as true and not concern ourselves with sacramental renewal? Because, if "Jesus Christ alone remains the first and enduring sacrament," we can ill-afford to neglect any opportunity to meet him. He is the one into whom we are baptized;

moreover, he is the host at the table. There, at font or pool and table, we particularly encounter the living Lord. Of course we can be Christians—even grow as Christians—without having a strong sacramental life. But why neglect means of grace that have brought nourishment and power to countless others for so long?

The Reasons We Neglect the Sacraments

In my pastoral experience, two reasons have often surfaced for our past sacramental laxity. One is *relational*, while the other is *educational*. The relational reason is less obvious, for it lies deep within us, encased in our life experiences. For example, some worshipers come to the table and are immediately turned off, yet they don't know why. They have been invited to the family meal or the holy meal or the feast of our Lord, but that very invitation triggers some deep and unpleasant memories the moment family meals or table are mentioned. Their memories kick into high gear and play back tapes long forgotten about their experience around the family table. If they ate at all with their families, the meals occurred in the middle of a family fight or cold silence. All of their earlier associations with meals and food are therefore unpleasant. No wonder the minister's invitation to yet another meal falls on deaf ears and unresponsive hearts!

Years ago Reuel Howe insisted that there is an intimate connection between food and love. Holy communion, he said, is "the sacrament of the common food and the uncommon love."[4] Thus, even the way we feed our babies begins to prepare them for communion! If we feed them lovingly, we begin to establish a connection between food and love that is later highlighted at the table. As remote as the relationship may seem, pastoral experiences occasionally bear out the truth of Howe's claim. Once these relational difficulties are "unpacked," persons can come to the table without encumbering baggage.[5]

Perhaps the educational reason is even more important than the relational for the decline of the sacraments. Clearly we have failed to teach their meaning and practice. Now that the sacraments have become more important to us, we are rushing to make up for lost time. However, we cannot blame our current laxity on those who still insist that the so-called sacraments are only ordinances. We too have to shoulder the responsibility for minimizing God's gifts.

The Sacraments Revisited

Commonalities in Baptism and the Lord's Supper

Classic definitions of sacraments abound. Sacraments, for example, are "signs and seals of the covenant of grace." A modern definition describes them as "communal events and sign acts through which God gives himself to us."[6]

Consider this expanded definition: Sacraments are ceremonial sign-acts—instituted by God, commanded by Christ, empowered by the Holy Spirit, and accompanied by preaching on the death and resurrection of Christ—that we observe when we gather as the community of the new covenant to celebrate God's gifts of grace to us, to have them sealed in our hearts, and to anticipate the time when Jesus will be Lord of all creation. Now note each part.

Sacraments are ceremonial sign-acts. In a sacrament, God, in the power of the Holy Spirit, takes a physical substance like water and gives it a spiritual meaning. Thus, water becomes a sign of something holy, set apart for God's use as an agent of cleansing and pardon. Likewise, God sets apart bread and wine to signify the broken body and shed blood of Christ for the forgiveness of sins.

Sacraments are instituted by God and commanded by Christ. We did not create the sacraments; God did through Christ. We hear Christ say, "Do this in remembrance of me" (1 Cor. 11:24). And also, "Go therefore and make disciples of all nations, baptizing them in the name of the Father and of the Son and of the Holy Spirit" (Mt. 28:19a).

Sacraments require God's Spirit to become effective. "The Holy Spirit is at work in the lives of people before, in and after their baptism," according to *Baptism, Eucharist and Ministry (BEM)*.[7] In the Lord's supper we also invoke the Spirit who alone can unite us in bonds of unbreakable love and lead us into "all justice, truth and unity."[8]

Sacraments are accompanied by preaching on the death and resurrection of Christ. Surprisingly to some, preaching and the sacraments go hand in hand, for each needs the other. An emerging ecumenical consensus holds that preaching should accompany both sacraments, especially the Lord's supper. *"The celebration of the eucharist properly includes the proclamation of the Word,"* states *BEM*.[9] Yet baptism, too, necessitates the preaching of the promises of God. Why this insistence on preaching at the sacraments? Why not simply allow them to speak for themselves by *enacting* the Word? Because preaching is needed to proclaim and explain the promises of God, just as the sacraments are needed to authenticate them to us. Catherine Gonzalez reminds us that the sacraments "keep preaching on target,"[10] for "the heart of the Gospel is the death and resurrection of Christ."[11] Without faithful preaching, we would celebrate the sacraments with less and less understanding.

Sacraments are celebrated when we gather as the community of the new covenant. "The community of the new covenant" is also a term drawn from *BEM.*[12] The new covenant is a covenant of grace, founded on Jesus Christ, who offered the gift of living water through his life, death, and resurrection. It is the *community* of the new covenant, sealed in Christ's blood, that was "poured out for many for the forgiveness of sins" (Mt. 26:28).

Of course, both baptism and the Lord's supper have meanings for the individual. After all, an *individual* is baptized, and the Lord's supper proclaims forgiveness of sins, including individual sins. Yet we come together as a *community* to celebrate both sacraments. We are not isolated individuals; we are part of the body of Christ. As we shall see, in our baptism we are incorporated into Christ and we are also incorporated into the body of Christ—the community of the new covenant. Affirming the public nature of baptism, James F. White declares: "The presence of a community of faith is almost as important as the use of water."[13] No more private baptisms!

Nor is the Lord's supper individualistic. At the table we renew our love and fellowship *with one another as members of Christ's body*. At the table we also remember the ties that bind us to our fellow Christians all over the world, regardless of gender, race, class, or nation.

So, both sacraments are sacraments of the *church*. Just as we do not baptize in isolation, we also do not celebrate the Lord's supper in isolation. Even when observing communion with shut-ins, some denominations insist that other members of the congregation should be present.

The sacraments celebrate God's gifts of grace to us. What are those gifts of grace? Specifically, God's promise to love us in Christ "while we still were sinners" (Rom. 5:8); God's promise to forgive us for our sins; and God's offer of new life in Christ. These overwhelming gifts are freely offered to all in the gospel. The sacraments are yet another way God offers us these gifts.

When we observe the sacraments, we emphasize what *God* has done more than what *we* must do. Not gifts that we can earn, the sacraments are means of grace to be received. Therefore, we always stress God's prior saving activity. Yet the benefits of the sacraments are not helpful to us apart from our response of *faith*. Even when we baptize a child, the person or persons assuming parental responsibility for the child must have faith.

The sacraments seal God's promises in our hearts. Modern packaging processes make it almost impossible for us to open any bottle of medicine now unless we break a seal. The seal ensures both the freshness and the safety of the product. A seal, however, can also guarantee the authenticity of a product. Some products bear the *Good*

Housekeeping seal of approval, which validates their quality. Thus, the sacraments of the church guarantee the promises that God makes in the gospel.

Still, the seal on any document is more than a sign. If I buy a piece of property, I receive a deed of trust, with all its official seals attached. All that the deed refers to is actually transferred to me and placed in my hands. "In the same manner," Catherine Gonzalez notes, "baptism and communion actually give to us what the Word proclaims. The promises are given to us, placed in our hands, transferred to us, personally and by name. We become a community of people who share in these promises."[14]

Finally, the sacraments *anticipate the time when Jesus will be Lord of all creation.* Each sacrament points to the "last things," when, as Paul said, "at the name of Jesus every knee should bend…and every tongue should confess that Jesus Christ is Lord, to the glory of God the Father" (Phil. 2:10, 11). Both baptism and the Lord's supper are imbued with this anticipation, looking toward the day when Jesus will be Lord of all creation.

In the meantime—between the *already* and the *not yet* of the kingdom—the sacraments call us to discipleship, witness, and service. From one standpoint we are relatively passive in the sacraments when we receive God's gifts: Someone puts water on my head or serves me bread and wine. But the sacraments also call on us to respond actively by putting our lives on the line for the gospel we have received. By so doing, we show the strength of the sacraments. They empower us for mission and lead us to work for justice and peace in a world that cries out for both.

The Lord's supper, for example, has the potential to bring us together around the table with strangers, enemies, and people of different classes and races. Our failure to embody this eucharistic ideal in most of our churches stands in sharp contrast with Jesus who "sat at dinner" with "tax collectors and sinners" (Mt. 9:10). So far, we haven't even been able to bring together fellow Christians!

We have noted the similar meanings baptism and the Lord's supper share. What are their distinctive meanings?

The Distinctive Meaning of Baptism

***"Baptism 'unites the one baptized with Christ…'* BEM states.** "[15] When we are baptized, we participate in the death and resurrection of Christ. Hear Paul: "Therefore we have been buried with him by baptism into death, so that, just as Christ was raised from the dead by the glory of the Father, so we too might walk in newness of life" (Rom. 6:4). *Our own death and resurrection are contained in our baptism.*

Baptism promises that Christ died our death for us, forgiving and freeing the "old self" from the power of sin. We start to live a new life in him, thus showing the beginning of resurrection in our lives. Still, elements of the "old self" cling to us and rise up to haunt us. Only by laying hold upon the constant forgiveness of Christ can we show that we are walking "in newness of life" (Rom. 6:4b). So the Christian life is a demonstration of dying to our old selves and being raised into new selves. Death *and* resurrection: Baptism signifies both.

"**Baptism unites the one baptized with Christ *and with his people.*"**[16] In other words, by being united with Christ, we are automatically united with the church, his body. Those who are baptized and subsequently take a long vacation from church fail to understand the meaning of baptismal water. How can anyone who is in Christ possibly not be in the church? In fact, baptism is a sign of our entrance into the church. It makes no sense to be baptized into Christ and then act as if we no longer need the church.

Yet some people say they can "believe without belonging." But when we are baptized, we are baptized by a community into a community. "For in the one Spirit," says Paul, "we were all baptized into one body—Jews or Greeks, slaves or free—and we were all made to drink of one Spirit" (1 Cor. 12:13). We are thus united with Christ and *with his people* forevermore.

Being united with Christ and his people implies—requires—confession of sin and pardon.[17] In Jerusalem, Peter preached, "Repent, and be baptized every one of you in the name of Jesus Christ so that your sins may be forgiven" (Acts 2:38a). Baptism signifies that we have repented and been cleansed from our sins. Washed clean, we begin anew. Therefore, why not repeat baptism every time we sin again? No, for as one denominational guide puts it, "The efficacy of Baptism is not tied to the moment when it is administered, for Baptism signifies the beginning of life in Christ, not its completion. God's grace works steadily, calling to repentance and newness of life. *God's faithfulness needs no renewal.* Human faithfulness to God needs repeated renewal."[18]

Although we can and do reaffirm the commitments made at our baptism, we are not rebaptized. That would say, "God, we didn't believe you the first time! Promise again!" But God's faithfulness to *us* needs no renewal. However, we often need to renew our faithfulness to *God.*

Water is the sign used in baptism. Water has tremendous value as a sign because it signifies the washing away of our sins. Whether we baptize by sprinkling, pouring, or immersion, we use water as an outward, visible sign of what God does for us inwardly to cleanse us from sin. What is not acceptable is baptism by *touching*!

Do we not need a sign-act to demonstrate that our sins have been washed away? We live in a world that denies the reality of sin, that blames everything on heredity or environment or education. *Au contraire!* Sin is a reality for all of us, because we thrust God from the center of our lives and fail to love our neighbors as ourselves.

The Distinctive Meaning of the Lord's Supper

The Lord's supper, like baptism, has several distinctive meanings. Each is significant.

The Lord's supper is a "thanksgiving to the Father," in the words of BEM.[19] The popular and cherished term *eucharist* is derived from the Greek word *eucharistia,* which means the "giving of thanks." When Jesus commenced the Last supper, he certainly "gave thanks." Even so, the New Testament does not specifically refer to the supper as the eucharist anywhere. Yet the supper *is* a joyful thanksgiving to God in which we proclaim and celebrate what God has done in creation, redemption, and sanctification.

What would it mean to our present communion observances if we infused them with a note of joy? Perhaps it would balance our sad, funereal services that speak only of the *death* of Christ. When we also recall the *resurrection* of Christ, we come to God in joyful thanksgiving.

Christ is particularly present at the table. But how? That is the question. Do the elements actually become the body and blood of our Lord as Roman Catholics contend? Is Christ present "in, with, and under" the bread and wine as Lutherans believe? Or is Christ really and spiritually present through the Holy Spirit as Presbyterians assert? Countless books explore how Christ is present, and your denomination has its own interpretation. Although perhaps no statement will ever fully resolve the dispute, *BEM* affirms what many Christians can accept: "The Church confesses Christ's *real, living and active presence* in the eucharist."[20] If most of us could agree on this statement, we might be able to reach consensus on other disputed points.

The supper "is the memorial of the crucified and risen Christ, i.e. the living and effective sign of his sacrifice."[21] The word *memorial*—also remembrance—is a translation of the difficult Greek word *anamnesis.* So used, however, memorial is far more than an event to keep the memory of Christ's death alive. For, in the words of Gregory Dix, it is "the 're-calling' before God of the one sacrifice of Christ in all its accomplished and effectual fulness so that it is here and now operative by its effects in the souls of the redeemed."[22]

Think of it! In the supper, through the Spirit, we can recall the past event of Christ's death with such power that the past becomes present. Whenever we gather at the Lord's table, Christ is present to forgive us, strengthen our faith, and equip us for service. This dynamic understanding of the eucharist has transformed the experience for many.

To understand the supper further, look at its roots in the Jewish Feast of the Passover in the Old Testament. When Christ said, "Do this in remembrance of me," he dramatically linked his supper with the Passover feast. Before the Lord's "pass over" of the Hebrew children, Hebrew families were supposed to slay a lamb and put some of its blood on the two doorposts and lintel. "The blood," said the Lord, "shall be a sign for you on the houses where you live: when I see the blood, I will *pass over* you, and no plague shall destroy you when I strike the land of Egypt" (Ex. 12:13, italics mine). Note verse 14: "This day shall be a day of remembrance for you. You shall celebrate it as a festival to the LORD."

Whenever Jews have observed the Passover, it has been more than a memory for them. They have become contemporaries with their forebears and have been saved from bondage along with them. Rabbi Gamaliel, explaining the Passover event in Exodus 13:8, said, "Every Israelite must know that he has been personally freed from slavery."[23] Thus, Jews to this day recall the Passover so that it becomes alive for them in the present moment.

But according to our Christian faith, the Supper that *we* now eat is the New Passover. At his Last Supper with his disciples, Jesus said he earnestly desired to eat this Passover with them. Yet he reinterpreted the Passover in terms of his sacrifice on the cross. "Do this *from now on*," he seemed to be saying, "as a memorial of *me*." *He* became the lamb of God who was slain for the sins of the world. As Paul said, "For our paschal lamb, Christ, has been sacrificed" (1 Cor. 5:7b). In the texts instituting the supper, Jesus used sacrificial language, saying, "This cup that is poured out for you is the new covenant in my blood" (Lk. 22:20; see also 1 Cor. 11:25). "In the context of the Passover festival," says James White, "one could not have signified sacrifice any more obviously to first-century Jews, for whom the covenant on Mt. Sinai was ratified by the pouring out of blood" (Ex. 24:6–8).[24]

Not only was Jesus the Lamb of God *slain*, but he is also the Lamb of God *standing* before God, pleading with God on our behalf, saying, "On the basis of what I have done, forgive them for their sins." The Lord's supper thus is a special way the past event of Calvary becomes present to us. Just as God delivered the Israelites from bondage to the Egyptians, so does God deliver us from bondage to our sins.

Do we repeat the sacrifice of Christ in the supper? No. Hear Calvin when he says that "the Lord's body was once for all so sacrificed for us that we may now feed upon it, and by feeding feel in ourselves the working of that unique sacrifice; and that his blood was once so shed for us in order to be our perpetual drink."[25]

Bread and wine are the signs God chose to signify God's self-giving in the death and resurrection of Christ. These common elements become a sign-act that is holy, for they point to the broken body and shed blood of Christ.

Remember that the bread and wine connect us to our Jewish roots. In fact, the tie is so strong that "Calvin could call the Passover meal a sacrament of the Old Covenant, along with circumcision."[26] At the Feast of the Passover, as God originally commanded, both bread and wine were significant. Jews ate unleavened bread because the deliverance from Egypt was accomplished in haste, suddenly, before the dough could even rise, and immediate obedience was necessary. Wine was also important to signify a renewal of the covenant and to celebrate their freedom. So whenever persons want to substitute pizza and Coke for bread and wine, they do not realize that they risk losing a valuable part of their heritage.[27]

The Redeemer Board Explores the Sacraments

Board members were astonished by the different understandings of the sacraments and also by their neglect of them. They resolved to remedy the situation, but concurred that it would take a long time. When they remembered the dynamics of change, they knew they needed to be patient, because the congregation would resist changing sacramental practice. Yet all were convinced that change was needed in order for them to experience the full benefit of God's gifts of grace. Soon they adopted an action plan to move them toward sacramental renewal. They

1. ***Asked the worship committee to develop policies for observing both baptism and the Lord's supper and to recommend any further liturgical changes that would highlight the importance of the sacraments.*** Pastor Justin said, "We need to adopt some sort of official policy for both sacraments. For example, people frequently make unusual requests about baptism. I've tried to honor every request, because I didn't want to offend anyone, especially a board member! It would help us to develop a common understanding of the practices we favor."

2. ***Requested the nurture committee to explore ways to teach the entire congregation the meaning of the sacraments.*** "This study is crucial," said Amanda. "We need to understand what our own denomination teaches about the sacraments, as well as what we can learn from the Christian tradition. It will be a revelation to our people."

Policies for Baptism and the Lord's Supper

Following the board's decisions, the worship committee went to work and gave its first report two months later. The proposed policies for baptism and the Lord's supper largely summarized the denomination's position on the sacraments. It was the board's responsibility to guide the congregation and to make decisions about administering the sacraments. The new baptismal policy, after explaining the sacrament, included numerous provisions:

1. Previous baptisms conducted in other denominations are valid as long as water was used and the baptism was in the name of the Father, of the Son, and of the Holy Spirit.

2. Requests for *repeat* baptisms will not be approved. (Rather, the policy explained why God's faithfulness needs no renewal in baptism.)

3. Special baptismal requests, such as baptizing with a rose dipped in the font or using water from the Jordan River, may be denied. (The policy explained that the rose detracted from the sign value of the water and that water from the Jordan River might be magically interpreted as being more effective than the water regularly used.)

4. All baptisms—adult and infant—will ordinarily be conducted during public worship. (Previously some baptisms had been scheduled after church for the convenience of some families. The new policy insisted on the communal nature of baptism, declaring baptism to be a sacrament of the whole church, because it celebrates our initiation into the church. Thus, the congregation needs to be present.)

5. Opportunities will be provided for church members to renew their own baptismal vows. (Committee members believed this action would reduce requests for rebaptism.)

The new policy adopted on the Lord's supper, after explaining the supper, contained several important provisions, which:

1. Instituted *monthly* communion on each first Sunday, and offered additional opportunities during special seasons like Lent and Advent. (A minority of board members favored *weekly* communion, remembering that Luther, Calvin, and Wesley had all favored weekly communion. However, a majority of board members spoke for monthly

communion, reminding the minority that none of the church fathers mentioned had been successful in perpetuating weekly communion among his followers! Of course, some traditions, including Catholic, Orthodox, Anglican, and Restorationist churches, have always practiced weekly communion.)

2. Stressed that the invitation to the supper would be extended only to baptized members. (This had occasionally been a problem at Redeemer Church whenever *baptized* children of church families invited *unbaptized* children to attend church with them. The policy noted that Christians move from font to table, and not the reverse, because baptism is the sign of entrance into the church. It explained that there is a process leading to baptism that should be followed before any candidate is baptized, whether a child or an adult. Candidates or their parent(s) should be instructed before engaging in baptism. Only after being initiated into the church through baptism should persons be nurtured in the faith by the supper.)

3. Reaffirmed bread and wine as the proper elements for the Lord's supper. (Jan explained that this policy needed to be reaffirmed because at a church family camping event last year pizza and Coke had been served. However, a motion to use fermented wine was defeated in spite of the biblical precedent for using it. The board decided that congregational and community reaction against wine would not be worth the conflict.)

4. Recommended *intinction* as an alternative way to receive the bread and the cup. (Previously people had been served only in their pews. The new option allowed them to come forward and dip the broken bread into the cup.)

Changes in Liturgy

The worship committee had already looked at the liturgy as a whole and carefully adopted a new liturgy. At that time the board did some preliminary work on the place of the sacraments in the liturgy. Now the committee's specific task was to enrich the congregation's practice of them. Jan, who chaired the committee, called on Pastor Justin to tell the board about their committee discussion.

"I've been thinking about how I might interpret the sacraments more effectively," Justin began. "I especially want to remember that both the sacraments and preaching deal with the death and resurrection of Christ—the heart of the gospel. Certainly I need to keep my preaching focused on the heart of the gospel. Then I can refer to the sacraments quite naturally as ways for us to enact the gospel."

"I also think," continued Justin, "that on a Sunday when a baptism is scheduled my sermon should definitely be related to baptism. And it would be wise to have the sermon before the baptism, just as we have done with the Lord's supper. The sacraments need to be interpreted often, and preaching is the preeminent way to interpret them. Incidentally, I promise to use more water when I baptize!"

"My concern," said Al, "is not with the changes you have proposed, but with the congregation's possible reaction when they haven't studied the sacraments as we have."

Teaching the Sacraments

Earlier, board members realized that one of the most important reasons congregations have historically neglected the sacraments is due to their failure to understand them. Thus, they saw how important it was to engage church members in the same kind of eye-opening study they had experienced.

"The possibilities are enormous," said Malcolm, as he began the nurture committee's report, "for teaching sacramental renewal to both adults and children. I've recently noticed that our Sunday school materials contain more references to the sacraments than ever before. So we want to encourage our teachers to use every opportunity to teach the meaning of the sacraments, using the materials they already have. However, some of our teachers have never studied the sacraments. So our first proposal is to provide four study sessions during our family night suppers this fall. That will give our teachers a chance to attend."

After discussion, Malcolm continued: "Another idea we favor is to give a candle to every newly baptized person. That's an ancient custom in which the candle given the candidate has been lighted from the paschal candle."

"Hold it," said Susan. "What's a paschal candle?"

"Early on," Malcolm replied, "the paschal candle was a sign of the death and resurrection of Jesus Christ and was central to the 'Easter vigil.' So it always remained near the communion table through the Easter season. It was lighted each Sunday from Easter through Pentecost Sunday. After Pentecost Sunday, it was placed beside the baptismal font and lighted only if someone was baptized. When candles were given to the newly baptized at their baptism, they were lighted from the paschal candle and given to the newly baptized or their parents. Then the minister said: "You have passed from darkness to light. Shine as a light in the world to the glory of God."

"We were thinking," added Maria, "that the candle custom could be very useful in helping people remember their baptism. On the anniversary of a family member's baptism, the candle could be lighted as part of family worship. Then the story of Jesus' baptism in Matthew 3:13–17 could be read and gifts of spiritual significance, like a Bible, could be given. Parents could also describe the occasion of the baptism to their child."

"We also thought," Malcolm said, "that our Sunday school teachers could send greetings to their students on the anniversary of their baptism. Perhaps they could mention it in class on Sunday morning. After all, baptism signifies our spiritual birth into the family of God. It ought to be even more important to us than our physical birthday celebration."[28]

"While we're at it," said Steve, "I think we should produce a kind of pastoral manual to guide our members at important times in their lives, such as confirmation and marriage, as well as baptism and the Lord's supper."

"Good idea," replied Justin. "I could then distribute the manual to all new members when they join our church, and we could also distribute it to the congregation at one of our family night dinners and discuss it for our program."

Although the committee had further ideas about the Lord's supper, it decided it had presented enough for one meeting. The process of sacramental renewal at Redeemer Church proved slow and required careful planning, but it proceeded well. After a year of education and interpretation throughout the church, church members began to rejoice at every baptism and to give heartfelt thanks to God at every communion service.

CHAPTER 9

Connecting the Functions through Small Groups

The Redeemer board had studied being, doing, telling, and celebrating the gospel and made numerous changes in the time I worked with them. Although we did not address every important area of church life, we agreed that these four traditional functions were significant ways to begin revitalizing their church. Only one thing remained on the board's wish list to discuss with me: small groups. While small groups may actually strengthen the being of the gospel more than doing, telling, and celebrating, they can offer a golden opportunity to connect all four functions.

When I called for discussion on the board's experience in small groups, Maria spoke first. "I grew up in a small, rural church in Ohio," she said. "In one sense my whole church was nothing but a small group! We were just one big family. Sometimes I've missed that family feeling in our larger church."

"I don't know much about small groups," Paul said, "but I do know that some of our members have asked me why we don't have a small-group ministry. One of them said she has to go to another church for small-group Bible study, and another person mentioned that he went to what he called a sharing group. Now, I'm not so much concerned that they went to other churches to meet some of their needs, but are we failing to provide for basic spiritual needs that people have?"

Responding quickly, Steve said, "I think we are. I was reflecting just the other day about how much I have learned about the gospel since I came on this board. The fellowship with all of you has been tremendous, and I know my faith has grown stronger. In a sense we have functioned as a small group. We have studied, prayed, served, and cried together. Why don't we provide similar opportunities for everybody?"

"I've been thinking along those same lines myself, Steve," Pastor Justin replied. "I've always been a strong believer in relationships as the primary way to experience God. When I was immersed in clinical pastoral education in seminary, I soon learned that ministry does not consist in accumulating a stockpile of pat answers to the vexing questions of life. Rather, I learned the value of offering caring and compassionate listening and 'staying with persons' in their intense struggles. That initial course led me to enroll in clinical pastoral education for a full year following graduation. That year in a small-group setting was a place for me to be who I really was. Sometimes I felt full of anger, hate, and doubt. At other times, I felt full of love, joy, and faith. I have often thought that, without that small-group experience in the course of that year, I might have left the ministry. So I would like to know how we can get started."[1]

Starting a Small-Group Ministry

Justin's question paved the way for us to explore the relation between small groups and the gospel. Strangely, it had never occurred to Justin before that a dynamic small group in the church might enrich the lives of many parishioners. In fact, such a caring place might even keep some of them from leaving the church. Although Justin himself had been deeply formed in a relational, small-group setting, he did not attempt to create small groups in the churches he served. Instead, he primarily stressed the relationship that existed between him and his people in one-on-one situations.

Part of my discussion with the Redeemer board dealt with how Jesus began his ministry—with a small group of twelve men whom he chose "to be with him" (Mark 3:14). After briefly presenting the dynamics of that group, I moved to Acts 2:42 and discussed the amazing events in Jerusalem soon after the gospel exploded and thousands of persons "devoted themselves to the apostles' teaching and fellowship, to the breaking of bread and the prayers" (Acts 2:42). Then I traced the small-group movement down to the present, highlighting everything from the Wesley bands to the fifty-thousand-member Yung Nak Presbyterian Church in Seoul, which is organized around small groups. The rest of what I told them forms the substance of this chapter.

When I reflect on forty years in ministry, I see that many of my deepest, most vital Christian experiences have occurred in small groups. I remember:

- the dynamic fellowship I had with a group of men in a Lynchburg, Virginia, church when we were learning person-to-person evangelism
- another group of men whom I met for breakfast every Saturday morning in Norfolk, Virginia, to pray for one another
- a "circle" of women I met with in Charlotte, North Carolina, to study how we could better understand the stresses and strains of everyday living
- a small group of persons I met with in Stone Mountain, Georgia, each week to practice various disciplines of the Christian faith
- numerous small groups of students who sat with me in my office at Columbia Theological Seminary to talk about their calls to ministry and their hopes and dreams for the future
- a group of students with whom I traveled to Central America for three weeks, struggling with issues of Christian witness and service amid poverty and international politics

In each case these groups were centers of power and new life. Yet small groups don't always turn out so well! A few of the most miserable experiences I have ever had occurred in small groups too. Someone dominated every discussion. Or wouldn't say anything. Or made sarcastic comments about everything that came up. Or was so nervous that it rubbed off on the rest of us. Or was so quiet that it became painful for the group.

At times I could have cut the tension with a knife. Or felt terribly threatened by what was happening. Or failed to confront persons who needed to become more accountable for their behavior because I wouldn't take the risk.

So I have no illusions about small groups. They can become vital centers of spiritual power or areas of frustration.

Still, a small group has more often than not been a source of power for me. But why? In that context, there's no pulpit or podium to hide behind. You sit down with others in an intimate setting to learn and grow. We are more likely to reveal who we really are in small groups than in large. Large groups tend to inhibit, even frustrate, us. Not everyone, of course. I know certain people who in every large church setting will almost surely speak—and often. Yet are not most people more inclined to speak and interact in a small group?

Of course, large groups have their place in the church. Conferences, conventions, stadium rallies, church services, and Sunday school classes will always provide the context for mobilizing and inspiring people the world over. Within the memory of most of us is a service in a crowded sanctuary or a lecture in a spacious auditorium that we'll never forget. Certainly we will continue to need large groups for what they alone can do.

Even so, small groups have been absolutely essential in the history of the Christian church. Now many predict that they will be even more necessary in the twenty-first century as we become increasingly immersed in a culture alien to the gospel. Christians will need a place to stand (or sit!) in the midst of culture to discover spiritual resources and experience the "communion of saints." And that is precisely what is happening now. When Jesus said, "For where two or three are gathered in my name, I am there among them" (Mt. 18:20), he gave us the very promise we need for the living of these days.

Current Trends

Sociologist Robert Wuthnow reports that an astonishing "four out of every ten Americans belong to a small group that meets regularly and provides caring and support for its members."[2] We are literally meeting everywhere to study the Bible, to support one another, to pray for one another, to plan ministry, to discuss the issues of today—the list goes on and on. *And these groups are changing the way we define spirituality and understand community.*[3]

While not all the small groups are intentionally Christian, many are. Members report that they feel closer to God, are better able to pray, are more interested in reading the Bible or other religious texts, and are more confident that they are acting according to spiritual principles that emphasize love, forgiveness, humility, and self-acceptance. Moreover, such groups provide people a sense of community in a society that has lost traditional support structures.

Thus, when we yearn to see a church revitalized, we dare not ignore the potential of small groups. Not only have they been vessels of the Spirit in the past, they are now offering numerous people both *community* and *spirituality*. Such benefits are well worth exploring.

But not so fast! Our commendation of small groups cannot turn into a money-back guarantee that they will promote both Christian community and an authentic spirituality. Sometimes they merely become communities for individualists. In other words, people in such groups may remain committed to them only as long as they find them personally helpful.[4]

Also, some small groups comfort persons without challenging them. Indeed, 82 percent of participants in small groups say "their group helps them feel that they aren't alone."[5] Yet is comfort all we need in the midst of struggle and pain? As important as comfort is, we also may need to confront our negative feelings about ourselves.

Note yet another caveat: Small groups can afford spiritual growth without roots. Unquestionably, small groups have helped members grow spiritually. Yet some groups fail to increase their members' knowledge of the Bible or theology. The only time such groups rely on the Bible or mention theology is to help members live better lives. To help people in their daily life is beneficial, but Wuthnow worries that those groups may be doing more to adapt religion to secular culture than to guide people to a deeper sense of the sacred.[6]

Surely, if small groups revitalize your church, you want them to do so by pointing members beyond their own individual needs to true *koinonia*—fellowship—in which the beliefs and origins of all are included and valued. You want to challenge members to look beyond their own need for support to the needs of the world. In the early church we cannot forget that there was "not a needy person among them" (Acts 4:34a). You want members of small groups, as they grow, to gain a greater awareness of the biblical and theological setting of the Christian story and how God has guided the church through the ages. As it was for the early church, is it not essential for us today to devote ourselves to "the apostles' teaching"? How else can we know that we are even growing as *Christians* unless we reflect on our life together in light of biblical teaching?

One thing more: I take quite seriously the importance for Christian small groups to meet in the power of the Spirit. We have seen that Jesus began his ministry in the power of the Spirit. Jesus promised his apostles that they would receive power to be witnesses when the Holy Spirit came upon them. Peter told the early Christians to repent and be baptized, saying to them, "you will receive the gift of the Holy Spirit" (Acts 2:38b). When they did repent and were baptized, they received the Holy Spirit with such power that they began to turn the world upside down. So, how can Christians meet for Bible study or prayer without seeking this same power? This power is none other than the presence of Jesus, the same presence promised when Jesus said, "For where two or three are gathered in my name, I am there among them" (Mt. 18:20). With that injunction clearly in mind, you can get started, believing that the

One who promised his presence in small groups also will guide you as you seek to develop them.

Doing Your Homework

Become familiar with basic resources. In addition to Wuthnow's foundational survey of small groups in *Sharing the Journey*, you will want to read a good book on biblical foundations. Such a resource is Gareth Weldon Icenogle's *Biblical Foundations for Small Group Ministry.* Icenogle thoroughly explores small groups, even saying that God lives in the Trinity as a small group![7]

With sociological, biblical, and theological foundations firmly in mind, next study a basic model for actually conducting a small-group study. Currently popular is Richard C. Meyer's *One Anothering.*[8] Around the theme of the "one another" passages in scripture—for example, "love one another"—Meyer suggests the content for an eleven-week study.

Also, you will need a book that helps you with the actual structure and dynamics of small groups. E. Stanley Ott's little book *Small Group Life: A Guide for Members and Leaders* effectively complements the material in the previous resources, telling you what to do and how to do it.[9] Put his book alongside the suggestions I make in the next section.

Now to this mix of resources add Dietrich Bonhoeffer's classic, *Life Together.*[10] The German martyr's intensely devotional description of what it means for Christians to live together in Christ will impress and inspire anyone who is interested in building Christian community. Who can forget Bonhoeffer's ringing affirmation that "Christianity means community through Jesus Christ and in Jesus Christ. No Christian community is more or less than this"?[11]

Participate in a small group yourself. Reading about groups from the perspective of the above authors is no substitute for actual experience. In such a setting you will see how it feels to be accepted or rejected, affirmed or ignored. Note how a good leader listens, then clarifies a point or extends the discussion. Observe what the leader does when the group falls silent. When conflict erupts, how does the leader handle it? Seminary students learn some of these skills in clinical pastoral education, but few seminaries require such courses. Hands-on learning helps plug the gap in a minister's preparation. While teaching courses in small groups over the years, I've often been surprised by how many ministers have never started a small-group program in their churches.

Study your context. Obviously, it would be ridiculous to recommend to Pastor Justin that he start a divorce recovery group if there were no divorced persons in his congregation. In a large church, however, such a group could offer the very setting in which many persons could rebuild their shattered lives.

In your work as a contextual sleuth, what root needs are you discovering? If parishioners want to grow but are not well-grounded in scripture, a Bible study group will prove helpful. If parents seem increasingly frustrated by the problems and demands of their families, a class on Christian parenting will give beleaguered parents the support and guidance they need. If the church lacks any understanding of the church's mission in the world, a ministry group organized around the three foci of study, fellowship, and mission provides a good launching pad.

In the absence of any conspicuous need, begin a basic small group on the "one anothering" passages, as Richard Meyer suggests. Concluding that group successfully will motivate you to try another. Starting a small group for the first time opens up a new world for many ministers.

Remember the essentials of small-group life. All groups need *clarity* about why they are meeting. When inviting people or announcing a small group, be specific about its purpose. Don't tell them you are meeting to study the Bible but then take up some other purpose. You may fool them once, but not twice!

Groups work better with a *covenant.* At the outset, go over ground rules about the time and length of meetings and any other principles that seem important. For example, establish a time for the group to conclude. That understanding will make a graceful exit possible for those who feel they want to do something else. Again, if you agree to keep all personal disclosures confidential, make sure that participants know the seriousness of this principle. When members fail to keep confidences, they not only block their progress—they may destroy the group.

Effective groups, of course, require *coordination.* Someone has to see that a meeting place is available, that people are reminded of any changes in times or dates, that leadership is in place, and that basic group needs are met. It's better to designate one coordinator than to rotate the responsibility.

Good groups need substantive *content.* Although a group may allow considerable latitude in discussing matters that surface, every group should build on solid content, whether the subject is Jeremiah or marriage enrichment. When groups meet only to "free associate," many people quickly lose interest.

Vital groups must develop good *communication.* This dynamic includes everything from reflective listening to confronting someone who is dominating the group and infuriating everyone else. Since many people avoid conflict, their group may disintegrate when no one is willing to hold the offending member accountable.

Healthy groups build their life around *Christ.* To underscore the point again, "Christianity means community through Jesus Christ and in Jesus Christ.[12] Church groups that want to develop true community and authentic spirituality must never forget the One in whose name they meet.

Finally, meaningful groups provide for good *closure.* If the group experience has been vital, then few persons will leave without some sadness, even genuine grief. And no wonder. The intimate setting has enabled them to move through various stages of group life, what has been called forming, storming, norming, performing, and mourning. Successfully negotiating the rapids of those stages with a group of people one has grown to love, trust, and respect is indeed significant. So give people a chance to express appreciation for one another, to shed tears, and to say good-bye.

One Pastor's Story

After my presentation, the Redeemer board seemed interested in beginning a small-group ministry. However, Jan spoke for the rest of the board when she said, "We've been doing many new things recently. So instead of being too ambitious, I think we ought to authorize Pastor Justin to start a pilot group at his convenience and to structure it as seems best to him. When he reports to us, we'll decide where to go from there."

"You would think that Jan and I set this up," laughed Justin. "But actually, we didn't. In my doctor of ministry program I signed up for a course in small groups. I wanted to discover the potential of 'people with people' groups, not just pastor with people one-on-one. A course requirement I most dreaded was starting a small group in my church. I would welcome this opportunity to do what Jan suggested...and also to finish this requirement!"

After studying his context, Justin decided to begin a small group on the theme of Advent, Christmas, and Epiphany. In his announcement he stated that the group would meet six times and be limited to twelve people. Eight persons signed up.

At the first meeting, Justin established a covenant among the group members. While they did not make a detailed covenant or put it in writing, they did agree to attend all the meetings and see the process through to the end. They also agreed to meet for only one hour and to start and end on time. As it turned out, all eight attended every meeting. However, Justin later regretted the one-hour restriction and intends to make his next group last an hour and a half. Too much raw human data poured forth to process in a one-hour session. The group also gladly embraced the confidential nature of the meetings.

A key dynamic that Justin included in his group was what Wuthnow calls "The Power of Stories."[13] In fact, storytelling has become the dominant mode of discourse in small groups. The stories we tell not only transform us into communal beings but also preserve our individuality. Is not each story we tell ours alone and subject to our own interpretations?[14] No wonder that three-fourths of members of small groups of all kinds say they have told personal stories in their groups at some time or another.[15]

Building, therefore, on the power of storytelling, Justin emphasized the importance of stories each time the group met. He modeled the principle by sharing some things about himself, often material he was later surprised he had revealed. Perhaps his vulnerability, plus the power of storytelling itself, triggered the flood of emotions the group unleashed.

For example, at one meeting Justin invited the group to talk about the memories they had of their fathers. He had based the lesson on Joseph, Jesus' father. Somehow the feelings evoked by discussing fatherhood seemed much deeper than the feelings evoked by motherhood in the previous session. One person wept during the whole session and chose not to share any memories about her father. Since the group was sensitive to her situation, no one put her on the spot. However, she later went to Justin and released all her conflicted, pent-up feelings about her father.

At another meeting a group member revealed that the death of her first husband had resulted from a self-inflicted shotgun blast to the chest. His suicide had occurred in another state, and she had remarried a person in Justin's church. No one in the group, including Justin, had ever been aware of her tragic story. Yet in that caring, trusting, and supportive atmosphere, she chose to reveal what she dared not disclose before.

When Justin concluded his group and reported to the board, he said, "The results have amazed me and caused me to give the small-group idea a deeper value in the life of the church."

Obviously surprised and pleased by his small-group experience, Justin said repeatedly that he felt he was standing on "holy ground" as members told their stories. Wrapping up his report, he said, "We had, as Bonhoeffer's *Life Together* suggests, achieved community—Christian community—'the communion of saints,' if you will."

The Redeemer board was so impressed by Justin's report that it voted to go forward with a small-group ministry. It authorized the fellowship committee to make plans to continue the good work Justin had begun.

Justin's small-group experience was not a momentary blip on the radar screen of church life today. It's happening in churches all across America. Many persons, meeting in small groups in the power of the Holy Spirit, are finding a place to belong. They are experiencing community "through Jesus Christ and in Jesus Christ." To be sure, these groups have their limitations and their critics. But I have seen them help revitalize churches. You can too!

Yet the starting line for revitalizing your board and congregation may not be small groups. Although critically important today, small groups will not work in some churches as well as others, nor are they a panacea for all that ails any church. You may see the four functions of the church coalesce around a service project as did the Westminster Presbyterian Church in chapter 4. Or they may center on dynamic worship that captures the interest and enthusiasm of your members. The Redeemer Church experience is therefore not limiting, only suggestive. The Spirit empowers different churches differently but always by equipping them with spiritual gifts to be employed for the common good. Your task is to find out how the Spirit has gifted you and then respond appropriately.

Of one fact I remain strongly convinced: Our churches will not be revitalized without the power of the Holy Spirit. For too long we have paid lip service to the Spirit but have not really sought the Spirit's power. Only by the Spirit's power will a church become a community. Only by the Spirit's power can we go about doing good as Jesus did. Only by the Spirit's power can we teach and preach the good news effectively. And only by the Spirit's power can we gather together to praise God and eat and drink with the Lord.

So wherever and whenever you start the renewal process in your church, begin by seeking the power of the Holy Spirit. God's spirit alone will renew our churches today when the fire goes out and they lag in zeal.

Appendix A

My Personal Rule of Life

Recognizing that I am baptized into Christ and into the church, Christ's body, I choose the following practices to help me grow in grace and to carry out my ministry.

Knowing the gospel (check those you feel led to do):

1. Daily I will study the scriptures to help me love, know, understand, and obey God.
2. I will study the tradition of my own denomination and that of the Christian church to discern God's action in history.
3. I will reflect on the daily news in light of the gospel of Jesus Christ.
4. I will take part in a discussion group dealing with current theological and ethical issues.

Celebrating the gospel (check those you feel led to do):

5. Daily I will offer my whole self to God in prayer, including feelings like anger, sadness, and doubt.
6. I will participate in a small group for sharing, study, and service.
7. I will share my faith as opportunities arise.
8. At least weekly I will worship with God's people, seeking every opportunity to celebrate the Lord's supper.

Being the gospel (check those you feel led to do):

9. Periodically I will take a spiritual inventory to explore who God wants me to be and how I am to live.
10. I will schedule quiet times for reflection and meditation, seeking to hear God speak to me.
11. I will cultivate my inner life by appreciating art, music, books, nature, and all the good gifts of God.
12. I will seek out a person or persons with whom I can discern the movement of God's spirit in my life.

Doing the gospel (check those you feel led to do}:

13. I will work in the world for justice and peace by becoming an advocate for victims of injustice and oppression.
14. I will think about the needs of the poor and take part in one ministry that serves them.
15. I will show my desire to live responsibly in all my relationships by spending more quality time with a family member.
16. I will serve as a faithful steward of God's creation by recycling and using other means of conservation.

Appendix B

Impediments to Spiritual Growth

First, write down your own thoughts about the kinds of things that seem to get in the way of prayer, worship, and meditation, or otherwise impede your development of spiritual awareness. Secondly, go over the list, checking those items that apply to you. See if you can think of any others. Next, write some comments about these blocks, and see if you can find a pattern in them and/or get in touch with some reasons that may underlie them. Finally, share your findings and reactions with another person.

No problems at all
Can't find the time
Other, more important things
Fear of losing control
Too tired usually
Can't concentrate
Feel tense, worried, afraid
Often fall asleep
Embarrassment
Can't stop thinking
Need to be logical
Can't give up control
Anger at church, God
Fear of God's judgment
Fear of God's demands
Fear God won't be there
Need to be *doing* something
Impatience
Feel selfish
Not comfortable physically
Can't think of words to pray
Afraid of failure
Feel no spiritual needs
Get bored, restless
It's too much work
Never get any results
Can't "just be"
Too much on my mind
Fear of giving up other things
Too many distractions
Don't know how to do it
Guilt or shame
Can't discipline self
Pride blocks me
Fear of being changed
Children, family demands
Disbelief that God is a Person to be talked to
Fear of fanaticism
Not comfortable mentally
Feeling lonely, no support

Adapted from Gerald G. May, *Pilgrimage Home: The Conduct of Contemplative Practice in Group* (New York: Paulist Press, 1979), 128.

Appendix C

Instructions for Conducting Home Meeting #1

Persons needed to conduct the meeting: host, moderator, devotional chairperson, and recorder.

1. Greet persons as they arrive and pass out name tags if persons do not know one another well.
2. Call on the devotional chairperson to give the opening devotional based on Galatians 6:1–10 or Romans 12:14–21.
3. Ask persons to introduce themselves, tell where they came from, and how long they have been members of your church.
4. Explain that the purpose of the meeting is to gather data from all members on how they see your church and community, including your strengths and resources as well as your needs, hurts, and hopes. Assure them that the data will be collated, meshed with data from other home meetings, and shared with them at a subsequent meeting.
5. Pass out a sheet titled "My View of the Church" and ask each person to fill it in without signing their names. (See the questions on page 34.)
6. Ask if some of them would like to share what they have written with the rest of the group. Spend time with each part of the "My View of the Church" instrument. Have the recorder list their comments on each part.
7. Now ask the group which concerns that they heard seem to be most important for each area. Have the recorder list those concerns.
8. Ask if anything else has occurred to them that they would like to add to their instruments before they hand them in. Tell them to indicate that those items were added later.
9. Ask them to hand in their sheets. Thank them for their cooperation. Announce the date of the follow-up meeting and ask the devotional chairperson to close with prayer.
10. Either the moderator or the recorder should turn in all the instruments plus the information recorded in numbers 6 and 7 above. Put the information in a folder, mark which home meeting was recorded, and turn it in to the church office as soon as possible. The pastoral care team will compile the data and it will be shared at the next meeting.

Appendix D

Instructions for Conducting Home Meeting #2

Persons needed to conduct the meeting: Same as #1.

1. Greet persons and pass out name tags if still needed.
2. Call on the devotional chairperson to give the opening devotional based on Romans 12:1–8.
3. Reintroduce persons, building on the previous fellowship.
4. Explain that the purpose of the meeting is to share the data gathered from the previous home meetings and to determine persons' interest in working with others to meet the needs of the congregation and the community.
5. Share the data collated by the pastoral care team, complete with notations about the material that was added when groups discussed how they had filled out "My View of the Church." Discuss and record the group's reaction to the data, including any new insights that emerge.
6. Now pass out a sheet titled: "My Response to the Needs of My Church and Community." Use the following questions.
   (a) With what specific needs of my church that have been identified am I willing to be involved? Please list.
   (b) How am I willing to be involved? Prayer? Financial support? Working with others in a ministry designed to meet that particular need? In some other way? Please underline each relevant answer and also explain in what other way you would be willing to participate.
   (c) What unmet community needs that have been identified especially invite me to participate? Please list.
   (d) How am I willing to be involved? Prayer? Financial support? Working with others in a ministry designed to meet that particular need? In some other way? Please underline each relevant answer and explain in what other way you would be willing to participate.
7. Ask them to discuss their responses and to add any additional thoughts that have occurred to them.
8. Ask them to turn in their responses and tell them that they will be contacted in the future. Thank them!
9. Either the moderator or recorder should turn in the sheets to the pastoral care team as soon as possible.

(See Kennon L. Callahan, *Twelve Keys to an Effective Church,* Chapter 1, for related information.)

Appendix E

The Mission of the Church in This Community and in the World

The closer your score is to agree or disagree the more intensely you agree or disagree. Pay attention to group scores that indicate high agreement or disagreement and also widely divergent scores. Discuss possible reasons for each.

I feel that

1. One of the major responsibilities of the church is to minister to persons' physical as well as spiritual needs.
   Agree _ _ _ _ _ _ _ Disagree
2. This church has clearly defined goals for its ministry to people in the the community and in the world.
   Agree _ _ _ _ _ _ _ Disagree
3. This church is now as active in ministering to the needs of others in this community and in the world as I would like it to be.
   Agree _ _ _ _ _ _ _ Disagree
4. The church has a responsibility to enable its members to minister to others in daily life.
   Agree _ _ _ _ _ _ _ Disagree
5. Participating in the life of this church significantly helps me fulfill my Christian responsibility in all of life.
   Agree _ _ _ _ _ _ _ Disagree
6. The church should be involved in social issues.
   Agree _ _ _ _ _ _ _ Disagree
7. I feel free to express my views on controversial issues to others in this church, even when they disagree with me.
   Agree _ _ _ _ _ _ _ Disagree
8. Ministers ought not to take stands on social issues when they know that many disagree with them.
   Agree _ _ _ _ _ _ _ Disagree
9. This church provides me with ample opportunities to minister to persons in the community and in the world.
   Agree _ _ _ _ _ _ _ Disagree

Appendix F

Reflections on the Present Service of Worship

1. Frequency with which I attend our services:
   Always____ Frequently____ Seldom____
2. What words would you use to describe our service?
3. If you were planning a new service, how would you like it to be different?
4. What part of our present service do you most appreciate? Why?
5. What feelings does the service typically arouse in you?
6. What thoughts or ideas or intentions do you most often leave the service with when you go home?
7. Other comments:

Do not sign your name.

Appendix G

Experiences with Contemporary Services

1. Expect opposition. Some will actively oppose the change and withhold pledges.

2. Create an orderly decision-making process. Involve as many people as you can in the planning process.

3. Gain support from church musicians. The principal opposition to the change may come from them, not from the leaders and congregation.

4. Turn out a good product. Boomers and busters expect high quality, so be prepared to invest some money.

5. Trust that the service will pay for itself. Most churches can reasonably expect an overall increase in attendance and a modest increase in financial support.

6. Be theologians. Do not automatically jettison the great hymns of the church! Remember that some contemporary hymns are "narcissistic, subjective, and individualistic."

7. Work for unity. Although creating a contemporary service inevitably causes some conflict, it can be overcome "through prayer, openness among the leadership and staff, clear communication, and fellowship opportunities shared by the whole congregation."

Adapted from Eric Snyder, "My Experience with Contemporary Services," *Monday Morning* 61, no. 11 (June 1996).

Appendix H

Reflections on Our New Service of Worship

1. Number of times you have participated in the new service: ____.
2. What words would you use to describe the services in which you have participated?
3. What, if anything, have you missed about the old service?
4. What have you most appreciated about the new service?
5. Would you like the new service to be different in still other ways? If so, how?
6. What are some of the feelings the new service has aroused in you?
7. What thoughts or ideas or intentions does the new service typically create in you?
8. Other comments:

Do not sign your name.

Notes

Introduction

[1] Lesslie Newbigin, *One Body, One Gospel, One World: The Christian Mission Today* (New York: Friendship, 1966), p. 20.

[2] Dietrich Bonhoeffer, *Life Together* (San Francisco: Harper & Row, 1954).

Part One: Revitalizing Fellowship

[1] Paul S. Minear, *Images of the Church in the New Testament* (Philadelphia: Westminster Press, 1960), 134.

Chapter 1. When Church Boards Become Faith Communities

[1] *Webster's New Twentieth Century Dictionary of the English Language* (New York: Simon & Schuster, 1979), 2043.

[2] I am almost certain that this research appeared in *Monday Morning: The Magazine for Presbyterian Leaders* sometime in 1996 or early 1997, but I have been unable to locate the issue.

[3] Corinne Ware, *Discover Your Spiritual Type: A Guide to Individual and Congregational Growth* (Washington: Alban Institute, 1995), 22.

[4] See my discussion of these characteristics in *Growing Church Leaders* (Decatur, Ga.: CTS Press, 1995), 5–8.

[5] Shirley C. Guthrie, *Always Being Reformed: Faith for a Fragmented World* (Louisville: Westminster John Knox Press, 1996), 85.

[6] Charles M. Olsen, *Transforming Church Boards into Communities of Spiritual Leaders* (Washington, D.C.: Alban Institute, 1995), 61.

[7] Thomas G. Long, "Myers-Briggs and Other Modern Astrologies," *Theology Today* 49 (October 1992), 291–95.

[8] See my *Growing Church Leaders,* especially chapters 1–3.

[9] Write to the Center for Parish Development, 5407 S. University Ave., Chicago, IL 60615 for more information about their work in servant leadership.

Chapter 2. Caregiving as a Sign of the New Reality

[1] See Paul Minear, *Images of the Church in the New Testament* (Philadelphia: Westminster Press, 1960).

[2] See Byron Kelley Bauknight's discussion in *Body Building: Creating a Ministry Team Through Spiritual Gifts* (Nashville: Abingdon Press, 1996), 28, 29.

[3] Ibid.

[4] Presbyterian Church (U.S.A.) *Book of Order*, G-6.0304. (Cited hereafter as *Book of Order.)*

[5] Ibid., G-6.042.

[6] Ibid., G-6.0304.

[7] See Jackson W. Carroll, Carl S. Dudley, and William McKinney, eds., *Handbook for Congregational Studies* (Nashville: Abingdon Press, 1986), 124.

[8] See Howard W. Stone, *The Caring Church: A Guide for Lay Pastoral Care* (San Francisco: Harper & Row, 1983), 37, 38.

[9] See Kenneth C. Haugk, *Christian Caregiving: A Way of Life* (Minneapolis: Augsburg, 1984); also see Kenneth C. Haugk and William J. McKay, *Christian Caregiving: A Way of Life: Leader's Guide* (Minneapolis: Augsburg, 1986).

[10] Stone, 37.

[11] Ibid., 38.

[12] Ibid., 39.

[13] For the basic outline of the principles of caregiving and understanding human behavior, I am indebted to the late William B. Oglesby, Jr., my mentor in pastoral care. The outline was derived in part from a retreat Oglesby led for the officers of Selwyn Avenue Presbyterian Church, Charlotte, N.C., when I was pastor.

Part Two: Revitalizing Service
Chapter 3. Service Inside the Body of Christ

[1] G. H. C. MacGregor, "The Acts of the Apostles," *The Interpreter's Bible,* (New York: Abingdon Cokesbury Press, 1954), 89.

[2] Carroll, Dudley, and McKinney, eds., 123–129.

[3] *Needs Assessment: An Exploratory Critique.* Office of the Assistant Secretary for Planning and Evaluation (HEW), Washington, D.C., U.S. Department, 1977.

[4] Hugh Anderson, James Cushman, Henry Snedeker-Meier, Bruce Tischler, and David Wasserman, contributors, *Congregational Mission Studies* (Louisville, Ky.: Evangelism and Church Development Ministry Unit, Presbyterian Church [U.S.A.], 1989).

[5] Carroll, Dudley, and McKinney, eds., 123.

[6] I wish to credit Amy Salmon, a student in one of my courses, for some of these ideas about AIDS. The ideas are drawn from a final project she wrote for P112: Introduction to Ministry, a course I taught with a team of teachers from Columbia Theological Seminary in Winter Park, Fla., in the fall of 1996.

Chapter 4. Service Outside the Church

[1] John W. Kennedy, "Candidates Court Family Values Vote," *Christianity Today* (7 October 1996), 80.

[2] Donald E. Messer, *Contemporary Images of Christian Ministry* (Nashville: Abingdon Press, 1989), 125.

[3] Ibid.

[4] Dieter T. Hessel, *Social Ministry: Revised Edition* (Louisville: Westminster John Knox Press, 1992), 221.

[5] Ibid., 102.

[6] *Book of Order,* G-1.0200.

[7] Cited in *Guide for Self-Evaluation.*

[8] Carl S. Dudley, *Action,* Jan.–Feb., 1989.

[9] Ibid.

[10] Carl S. Dudley, "Launching Social Ministries" *Church and Community Forum* 1, no. 1 (November 1990), 4.

[11] Ibid.

[12] Chris Burritt, "Protesters vs. profits," *The Atlanta Constitution,* 17 April 1997, Sec. A8.

[13] *Book of Order,* W-7.4002.

[14] Ibid., W-7.4001.

[15] The story of Westminster Presbyterian Church's service project was related in a paper that Mary Villilo wrote for P112: Introduction to Ministry, a course I taught with a team of teachers from Columbia Theological Seminary in Winter Park, Fla., in the fall of 1996.

[16] Olsen, 73, 74.

[17] Ibid., 73. These three questions were adapted by Olsen from Walter Wink, *The Bible in Human Transformation* (Philadelphia: Fortress, 1973).

Part Three: Revitalizing Proclamation

[1] C. H. Dodd, *The Apostolic Preaching and its Developments* (New York and London: Harper & Brothers, 1951).

[2] Richard Robert Osmer, *A Teachable Spirit: Rediscovering the Teaching Office in the Church* (Louisville: Westminster/John Knox Press, 1990), 15.

[3] Ibid., 64, 65.

Chapter 5. Nurture: Growing in the New Reality

[1] C. Ellis Nelson, "Christian Education in a Secular Society," *The Presbyterian Outlook* (25 April 1994), 6, 7.

[2] Ibid., 6.

[3] Ibid. Benton Johnson, Dean Hoge, and Donald Luidens, *First Things*, March 1993, quoted by Nelson, 6.

[4] Ibid., 6.

[5] Ibid.

[6] James Smart, quoted by Sara Little, "The Shifting Scene in Christian Education," *The Presbyterian Outlook* (28 April 1997), 12.

[7] Osmer, 179.

[8] Ibid., 180.

[9] Maria Harris, "Teaching: Forming and Transforming Grace," in *Congregations: Their Power to Form and Transform*, ed. C. Ellis Nelson (Atlanta: John Knox, 1988), 262.

[10] Tex Sample, *Ministry in an Oral Culture: Living with Will Rogers, Uncle Remus & Minnie Pearl* (Louisville: Westminster John Knox Press, 1994), 19.

[11] Charles R. Foster, "Communicating," in *Congregations: Their Power to Form and Transform*, 221.

[12] Erik H. Erikson, *Childhood and Society* (New York: W. W. Norton, 1964), 249; also see the rest of the chapter.

[13] Ibid., 250.

[14] Nelson, "Christian Education in a Secular Society," 7.

[15] Gay Mothershed, "Mothershed's Response to 'Christian Education in a Secular Society,'" *The Presbyterian Outlook* (25 April 1994), 17.

[16] Abraham Heschel, quoted by David F. White and Frank Rogers, "Existentialist Theology and Religious Education," ed. Randolph Crump Miller, *Theologies of Religious Education* (Birmingham, Ala.: Religious Education Press, 1995), 189.

[17] Donald W. Shriver, Jr., quoted in Forster Freeman, *Readiness for Ministry Through Spiritual Direction* (Washington, D.C.: Alban Institute, 1986), 16.

[18] Paul M. Dietterich, "Learning as a Communal Endeavor," *Transformation* 2, no. 3 (Summer 1995), 2.

[19] Ibid.

[20] Dale A. Ziemer, "Cultivating a Learning Community," *Transformation* 2, no. 3 (Summer 1995), 10.

[21] For more information contact the Center for Parish Development, 5407 S. University Ave., Chicago, IL 60615.

[22] Sample, 6.

[23] Ibid., 48.

[24] Ibid., 55.

[25] Nelson, "Christian Education in a Secular Society," 7.

[26] Carlyle Marney, *Priests to Each Other* (Valley Forge: Judson Press, 1978), 62.

[27] Nelson, "Christian Education in a Secular Society," 7.

[28] Marney, 62.

[29] Arthur R. Hall, "Book of the Week," *The Presbyterian Outlook* (5 February, 1996), 9. Hall was reviewing *The Trivialization of God: The Dangerous Illusion of a Manageable Deity* by Donald W. McCullough, Navpress, 1995.

[30] See William C. Placher, *Domesticating the Transcendence of God* (Louisville: Westminster John Knox Press, 1995).

[31] Carroll, Dudley, and McKinney, 138.

[32] The video *Signs of the Times: Reading Our Culture with Eyes of Faith* can be ordered from CTS Press, P.O. Box 520, Decatur, GA 30031.

[33] *Parenting for Life* by Penny Hill can be ordered from Essential Media Services, 805-489-1201.

[34] For information about Willimon's course *Making Disciples: A New Approach to Confirmation*, write Logos Productions Inc., 6160 Carmen Avenue East, Inver Grove Heights, MN 55076-4422.

[35] See Neil MacQueen, "In Their Own Language—Kids, Computers and Christian Education," *The Presbyterian Outlook*, 6, no. 7 (28 April 1997).

[36] David W. McCormick, "Neighborhood School of the Arts: A Church-Sponsored, Community-Based Educational Outreach," *The Presbyterian Outlook* (28 April 1997), 9.

[37] See Mary-Ruth Marshall, "The Shifting Scene in Youth Ministry," *The Presbyterian Outlook* (28 April 1997), 8, 10.

Chapter 6. Renewal through Preaching the New Reality

[1] Katrina Burger, "JesusChrist.com" *Forbes* (5 May 1997), 76.

[2] Tex Sample, lecture at Ginter Park Presbyterian Church, Richmond, Va., Winter, 1996.

[3] Tex Sample, *Ministry in an Oral Culture: Living with Will Rogers, Uncle Remus, and Minnie Pearl* (Louisville: Westminster/John Knox Press, 1994), 6.

[4] Ibid.

[5] Ibid., 11.

[6] Lucy Atkinson Rose, *Sharing the Word: Preaching in the Roundtable Church* (Louisville: Westminster John Knox Press, 1997), 37.

[7] Ibid., 37, for a good summary.

[8] Ibid, 60.

[9] Fred B. Craddock, *As One Without Authority: Essays on Inductive Preaching,* Revised Edition (Enid, Okla.: Phillips University Press, 1974), 59; quoted in Rose, *Sharing the Word*, 62.

[10] See Rose, 62.

[11] For further information on my view of servant leadership, see *Growing Church Leaders: New Skills for New Tasks* (Decatur, Ga.: CTS Press, 1995) and *The Pastor's Start-Up Manual: Beginning a New Pastorate* (Nashville: Abingdon Press, 1995).

[12] See John S. McClure, *The Roundtable Pulpit: Where Leadership and Preaching Meet* (Nashville: Abingdon Press, 1995).

[13] See Rose, *Sharing the Word.*

[14] Walter Brueggemann, *Preaching as a Social Act: Theology and Practice,* ed. Arthur Van Seters (Nashville: Abingdon Press, 1988), 137; quoted in Rose, *Sharing the Word*, 79.

[15] McClure, 60.

[16] Elisabeth Schüssler Fiorenza, in *A New Look at Preaching, Good News Studies,* vol. 7. ed. John Burke, 43–55. (Wilmington, Del.: Michael Glazier, 1983), 45, 49, 52; quoted in Rose, *Sharing the Word,* 125.

[17] McClure, 72.

[18] William H. Willimon, *Integrative Preaching: The Pulpit at the Center,* ed. William D. Thompson (Nashville: Abingdon, 1981), 31; Abingdon Preacher's Library.

[19] Reuel L. Howe, *Partners in Preaching: Clergy and Laity in Dialogue* (New York: Seabury Press, 1967), 96, 97. (These questions modified Howe's language somewhat.)

[20] Ibid., 102.

[21] See Rose, 127, for a helpful discussion of this point.

[22] Sample, 75.

[23] Katherine Paterson, *The Spying Heart: More Thoughts on Reading and Writing Books for Children* (New York:Lodestar Books, E. P. Dutton, 1989), 137; quoted in Rose, *Sharing the Word,* 125.

[24] *Book of Order,* W-2.2010.

[25] Ibid.

[26] Ibid., W-2.008.

[27] Sample, in a lecture at Ginter Park Presbyterian Church, Richmond, Va., quoting someone whose full name was lost in transmission.

[28] Sample, *Ministry in an Oral Culture,* 23.

[29] McClure, 60–72. I revised and fleshed out McClure's points.

Part Four: Revitalizing Celebration

[1] G. Abbott-Smith, *A Manual Greek Lexicon of the New Testament* (Edinburgh: T. & T. Clark, 1948), 266.

[2] John S. Groenfeldt, *We Gather Together: The Church Worships God* (Richmond: CLC Press, 1971), 23.

Chapter 7. Worship: Renewing Liturgy

[1] Marva J. Dawn, *Reaching Out without Dumbing Down: A Theology of Worship for the Turn-of-the-Century Culture* (Grand Rapids: Eerdmans, 1995), 3.

[2] James F. White, *Protestant Worship: Traditions in Transition* (Louisville: Westminster/John Knox Press, 1989), 15.

[3] C. C. Richardson, "Worship in New Testament Times, Christian," *The Interpreter's Dictionary of the Bible* (Nashville, New York: Abingdon Press, 1962), 883.

[4] Ibid.

[5] Ibid., 888, 889.

[6] White, 212.

[7] Dawn, 236.

[8] Ibid.

[9] Ibid., 206.

[10] "There is a Balm in Gilead," *The Presbyterian Hymnal* (Louisville: Westminster/ John Knox Press, 1990), no. 394.

[11] Theodore W. Jennings, Jr., *The Liturgy of Liberation: The Confession and Forgiveness of Sins* (Nashville: Abingdon Press, 1988), 17; quoted by Inagrace T. Dietterich, "Cultivating the People of God: Ecclesial Practices 2: Disciples Break Bread Together," *The Center Letter* 24, no. 6 (June 1994).

[12] Ibid.

[13] Ibid., see Inagrace Dietterich's discussion of this point.

[14] See *Book of Order,* W-1.4001.

[15] Richardson, 887.

[16] See Groenfeldt, *We Gather Together,* 13, for his discussion of this point.

[17] John H. Leith, *Introduction to the Reformed Tradition* (Atlanta: John Knox Press, 1977), 172, 173.

[18] Dr. Russell Stevenson, "What Is Presbyterian Worship? What Is Biblical Worship?" Unpublished paper, First Presbyterian Church, Baton Rouge, La., 1995; quoted by Stephanie D. Hankey in a paper written for a course I taught at Columbia Theological Seminary in the fall of 1995.

[19] Leith, 173.

[20] See Lyle E. Schaller, *The Change Agent: The Strategy of Innovative Change* (Nashville: Abingdon Press, 1972), 34ff.

[21] White, 33.

[22] *Book of Order,* W-2.1004.

[23] Dawn, 202.

[24] Ibid., 204.

[25] Kennon L. Callahan, *Dynamic Worship: Mission, Grace, Praise, and Power* (San Francisco: Harper, 1994), 30. Readers will profit from reading Callahan's other ideas on creating dynamic worship, but it is beyond the scope of this book to pursue such related subjects as worship options.

[26] Some of these ideas on change were adapted from Robert H. Ramey, Jr., *The Pastor's Start-Up Manual,* 74–78.

Chapter 8. Renewing the Sacraments

[1] Laurence Hull Stookey, *Eucharist: Christ's Feast with the Church* (Nashville: Abingdon Press, 1993), 59.

[2] Ibid.

[3] White, *Protestant Worship,* 211, 212.

[4] Reuel L. Howe, *Man's Need and God's Action* (Greenwich: Seabury Press, 1953), 84.

[5] Ibid., 83–86.

[6] William H. Willimon, *Worship as Pastoral Care* (Nashville: Abingdon Press, 1979), 149, 150. His statement is a paraphrase from James F. White, *Christian Worship in Transition* (Nashville: Abingdon Press, 1976), 42–51.

[7] *Baptism, Eucharist and Ministry* (Geneva: World Council of Churches, 1982), 2. Hereafter, cited as *BEM.*

[8] Ibid., 13.

[9] Ibid., 12.

[10] Catherine G. Gonzalez, *A Theology of the Lord's Supper* (Atlanta: General Assembly Mission Board, 1981), 7.

[11] Ibid., 6.

[12] *BEM,* 13.

[13] James F. White, *Sacraments as God's Self Giving* (Nashville: Abingdon Press, 1983), 127.

[14] Gonzalez, 7, 8.

[15] *BEM,* 2.

[16] Ibid., 2.

[17] Ibid.

[18] *Book of Order,* W-2.3007.

[19] *BEM,* 10, italics mine.

[20] Ibid., 12, italics mine.

[21] Ibid., 11.

[22] Gregory Dix, *The Shape of the Liturgy* (New York: The Seabury Press, 1982), 243, italics mine.

[23] Gamaliel, source untraced.

[24] White, *Sacraments,* 57.

[25] John Calvin, *Institutes of the Christian Religion,* McNeill-Battles translation, IV, xvii, 1.

[26] Gonzalez, 15.

[27] Ibid., see the discussion on page 15.

[28] Material adapted from *Holy Baptism and Services for the Renewal of Baptism: Supplemental Liturgical Resource* 2 (Philadelphia: Westminster Press, 1985), 60–62.

Chapter 9. Connecting the Functions through Small Groups

[1] The story of the formation of this small group is true; however, for obvious reasons, I have omitted the names of the minister and the church to protect their confidentiality.

[2] Robert Wuthnow, *Sharing the Journey: Support Groups and America's New Quest for Community* (New York: Free Press, 1994), 4.

[3] Ibid., 3.

[4] Robert Wuthnow, quoted in Eugene C. Roehlkepartain, "Where 2 or 3 Gather...," *The Christian Ministry* (May-June 1995), 7.

[5] Ibid.

[6] Ibid.

[7] Gareth Weldon Icenogle, *Biblical Foundations for Small Group Ministry: An Integrational Approach* (Downers Grove, Ill.: InterVarsity Press, 1994), 21.

[8] Richard C. Meyer, *One Anothering* (New York: Innisfree Press, 1990).

[9] E. Stanley Ott, *Small Group Life: A Guide for Members and Leaders* (Decatur, Ga.: CTS Press, 1994).

[10] Dietrich Bonhoeffer, *Life Together* (San Francisco: Harper San Francisco, 1978).

[11] Bonhoeffer, *Life Together,* 21.

[12] Ibid.

[13] Wuthnow, *Sharing the Journey,* 289.

[14] Ibid., 293.

[15] Ibid., 296.